Sixth International Workshop on Natural Language Processing for Social Media (SocialNLP 2018)

Held at ACL 2018

Melbourne, Australia
20 July 2018

ISBN: 978-1-5108-6722-2

ACL 2018

Natural Language Processing for Social Media

Proceedings of the Sixth Workshop
AFNLP SIG SocialNLP

ACL 2018 Workshop
July 20, 2018
Melbourne, Australia

SocialNLP 2018@ACL Chairs' Welcome

It is our great pleasure to welcome you to the Sixth Workshop on Natural Language Processing for Social Media-SocialNLP 2018, associated with ACL 2018. SocialNLP is an inter-disciplinary area of natural language processing (NLP) and social computing. We hold SocialNLP twice a year: one in the NLP venue, the other in the associated venue such as those for web technology or artificial intelligence. There are three plausible directions of SocialNLP: (1) addressing issues in social computing using NLP techniques; (2) solving NLP problems using information from social media; and (3) handling new problems related to both social computing and natural language processing. Through this workshop, we anticipate to provide a platform for research outcome presentation and head-to-head discussion in the area of SocialNLP, with the hope to combine the insight and experience of prominent researchers from both NLP and social computing domains to contribute to the area of SocialNLP jointly. The submissions to this year's workshop were again of high quality and we had a competitive selection process. We received submissions from Asia, Europe, and the United States, and due to a rigorous review process, we only accepted 7 long oral papers among 19. Thus the acceptance rate was 37 percent. In addition, we are having our first research challenge: EmotionX in the SocialNLP workshop. A total of 18 groups registered for the dataset and at last 5 groups submitted their results successfully. Therefore these year we have 7 research papers, 1 challenge overview paper as well as 5 challenge papers, that is, a total of 13 papers published in the proceedings of the ACL chapter for the SocialNLP 2018 workshop.

This year, we are excited to have Dr. Saif Mohammad from National Research Council Canada, and Dr. Yi-Chia Wang from Uber as our keynote speakers. We also encourage attendees to attend the keynote talk presentations to have more discussions with outstanding researchers. Their valuable and insightful talk can and will guide us to a better understanding of the future. Putting together SocialNLP 2018 was a team effort. We first thank the authors for providing the quality content of the program. We are grateful to the program committee members, who worked very hard in reviewing papers and providing feedback for authors. Finally, we especially thank the Workshop Committee Chairs Prof. Brendan O'Connor and Prof. Eva Maria Vecchi.

We hope you join our community and enjoy the workshop!

Organizers

Lun-Wei Ku, Academia Sincia, Taiwan
Cheng-Te Li, National Cheng Kung University, Taiwan

Organizers

Lun-Wei Ku, Academia Sincia, Taiwan
Cheng-Te Li, National Cheng Kung University, Taiwan

Program Committee:

Sabine Bergler, Concordia University
Yung-Chun Chang, Taipei Medical University
Hsin-Hsi Chen, National Taiwan University
Freddy Chua, Singapore Management University
Danilo Croce, University of Roma, Tor Vergata
Lei Cui, Microsoft Research
Ronan Cummins, University of Cambridge
Min-Yuh Day, Tamkang University, Taiwan
Ann Devitt, Trinity College Dublin
Koji Eguchi, Kobe University
Michael Elhadad, Ben-Gurion University
Wei Gao, Qatar Computing Research Institute
Spandana Gella, University of Edinburgh
Weiwei Guo, LinkedIn
William Hamilton, Stanford University
Graeme Hirst, University of Toronto
Wen-Lian Hsu, Academia Sinica
Hen-Hsen Huang, National Taiwan University
Diana Inkpen, University of Ottawa
David Jurgens, Stanford University
Roman Klinger, University of Stuttgart
Tsung-Ting Kuo, University of California, San Diego
Cheng-Te Li, National Cheng Kung University
Chuan-Jie Lin, National Taiwan Ocean University
Shou-De Lin, National Taiwan University
Zhiyuan Liu, Tsinghua University
Bin Lu, Google Inc.
Zhunchen Luo, China Defense Science and Technology Information Center
Bruno Martins, University of Lisbon
Yelena Mejova, Qatar Computing Research Institute
Rada Mihalcea, University of Michigan
Manuel Montes-y-Gómez, INAOE, Mexico
Dong Nguyen, University of Twente
Haris Papageorgiou, ATHENA Research and Innovation Center
Georgios Petasis, NCSR "Demokritos"
Stephen Pulman, Oxford University
Saurav Sahay, Intel Labs
Mário J. Silva, Universidade de Lisboa
Yanchuan Sim, Institute for Infocomm Research
Jan Snajder, University of Zagreb
Xavier Tannier, Université Paris-Sud, LIMSI, CNRS

Mike Thelwall, University of Wolverhampton
Ming-Feng Tsai, National Chengchi University
Svitlana Volkova, PNNL
Xiaojun Wan, Peking University
Hsin-Min Wang, Academia Sinica
Jenq-Haur Wang, National Taipei University of Technology
William Yang Wang, UC Santa Barbara
Ingmar Weber, Qatar Computing Research Institute, HBKU
Shih-Hung Wu, Chaoyang University of Technology
Ruifeng Xu, Harbin Institute of Technology
Yi Yang, Georgia Tech
Liang-Chih Yu, Yuan Ze University
Zhe Zhang, IBM Watson

Keynote Speaker:

Saif Mohammad, National Research Council Canada
Yi-Chia Wang, Uber

Challenge Chair:

Chao-Chun Hsu, Academia Sinica
Lun-Wei Ku, Academia Sinica

Keynote Speech I

The Search for Emotions, Creativity, and Fairness in Language

Speaker: Saif M. Mohammad, Senior Research Scientist, National Research Council Canada

Abstract: Emotions are central to human experience, creativity, and behavior. They are crucial for organizing meaning and reasoning about the world we live in. They are ubiquitous and everyday, yet complex and nuanced. In this talk, I will describe our work on the search for emotions in language – by humans (through data annotation projects) and by machines (in automatic emotion detection systems).

I will outline ways in which emotions can be represented, challenges in obtaining reliable annotations, and approaches that lead to high-quality annotations. The lexicons thus created have entries for tens of thousands of terms. They provide fine-grained scores for basic emotions as well as for valence, arousal, and dominance (argued by some to be the core dimensions of meaning). They have wide-ranging applications in natural language processing, psychology, social sciences, digital humanities, and computational creativity. I will highlight some of the applications we have explored in literary analysis and automatic text-based music generation. I will also discuss new sentiment analysis tasks such as inferring fine-grained emotion intensity and stance from tweets, as well as detecting emotions evoked by art. I will conclude with work on quantifying biases in the way language is used and the impact of such biases on automatic emotion detection systems. From social media to home assistants, from privacy concerns to neuro-cognitive persuasion, never has natural language processing been more influential, more fraught with controversy, and more entrenched in everyday life. Thus as a community, we are uniquely positioned to make substantial impact by building applications that are not only compelling and creative but also facilitators of social equity and fairness.

Bio: Dr. Saif M. Mohammad is Senior Research Scientist at the National Research Council Canada (NRC). He received his Ph.D. in Computer Science from the University of Toronto. Before joining NRC, Saif was a Research Associate at the Institute of Advanced Computer Studies at the University of Maryland, College Park. His research interests are in Emotion and Sentiment Analysis, Computational Creativity, Psycholinguistics, Fairness in Machine Learning, Crowdsourced Human Annotations, Social Media Language, and Information Visualization. Saif is a co-organizer of WASSA (a sentiment analysis workshop) and co-chair of SemEval (the largest platform for semantic evaluations). He has also served as the area chair for Sentiment Analysis in ACL conferences. His work on emotions has garnered media attention, with articles in Time, Washington Post, Slashdot, LiveScience, The Physics arXiv Blog, PC World, Popular Science, etc. Webpage: http://saifmohammad.com

Keynote Speech II

Understanding Online Social Behaviors
through Automatic Language Analysis

Speaker: Yi-Chia Wang, Data Scientist, Uber

Abstract: In online environments, people accomplish their social goals through the use of language - for example, presenting themselves appropriately on social networking sites, attracting followers in social media, or eliciting support in health support groups. In order to understand how people accomplish these goals and further design interventions to help people achieve them, we need sophisticated and scalable approaches to language analysis. My research investigates communication dynamics in online social environments. The goal is to understand how people use language to communicate with others online and its social outcomes, how language presentations are different in various types of online environments and provide guidance for practitioners to improve their services.

In this talk, I will present studies examining user behaviors in online environments. My research method consists of two phases: (1) developing machine learning models to automatically measure language concepts and (2) applying the models to analyze text at scale and quantitatively relate language concepts to user behaviors. The presentation will cover how I applied a similar research method to answer very different research questions and provide implications for practitioners.

Bio:

Yi-Chia Wang received her Ph.D. from the Language Technologies Institute in School of Computer Science at Carnegie Mellon University. Her research interests and skills are to combine language processing technologies, machine learning methodologies, and social science theories to statistically analyze large-scale data and understand user behaviors in online environments. Her thesis developed a machine learning model to study self-disclosure on Facebook. She also had experience on question answering and information extraction. She is currently a Data Scientist at Uber, focusing on customer support and conversational AI domains.

Table of Contents

Conference Program

July 20, 2018

09:20–10:30 *Keynote Speech (I):The Search for Emotions, Creativity, and Fairness in Language*
Dr. Saif Mohammad (NSF)

10:30–11:00 Coffee Break

11:00–12:20 Technical Session 1

Sociolinguistic Corpus of WhatsApp Chats in Spanish among College Students
Alejandro Dorantes, Gerardo Sierra, Tlauhlia Yamín Donohue Pérez, Gemma Bel-Enguix and Mónica Jasso Rosales

A Crowd-Annotated Spanish Corpus for Humor Analysis
Santiago Castro, Luis Chiruzzo, Aiala Rosá, Diego Garat and Guillermo Moncecchi

A Twitter Corpus for Hindi-English Code Mixed POS Tagging
Kushagra Singh, Indira Sen and Ponnurangam Kumaraguru

Detecting Offensive Tweets in Hindi-English Code-Switched Language
Puneet Mathur, Rajiv Shah, Ramit Sawhney and Debanjan Mahata

12:20–13:20 Lunch

13:20–14:30 *Keynote Speech (II): Understanding Online Social Behaviors through Automatic Language Analysis*
Dr. Yi-Chia Wang (Uber)

16:00–17:00   Technical Session 2

Towards Automation of Sense-type Identification of Verbs in OntoSenseNet
Sreekavitha Parupalli, Vijjini Anvesh Rao and Radhika Mamidi

Improving Classification of Twitter Behavior During Hurricane Events
Kevin Stowe, Jennings Anderson, Martha Palmer, Leysia Palen and Ken Anderson

Political discourse classification in social networks using context sensitive convolutional neural networks
Aritz Bilbao-Jayo and Aitor Almeida

17:00–17:10   Closing

Sociolinguistic Corpus of WhatsApp Chats in Spanish among College Students - Data Paper

Alejandro Dorantes   **Gerardo Sierra**   **Yamín Donohue Pérez**
Gemma Bel-Enguix   **Mónica Jasso Rosales**
Universidad Nacional Autónoma de México
Grupo de Ingeniería Lingüística
{MDorantesCR,GSierraM,TDonohueP,GBelE,MJassoR}@iingen.unam.mx

Abstract

The aim of this paper is to introduce the Sociolinguistic Corpus of WhatsApp Chats in Spanish among College Students, a corpus of raw data for general use, which was collected in Mexico City in the second half of 2017. This with the purpose of offering data for the study of the singularities of language and interactions via Instant Messaging (IM) among bachelors. This article consists of an overview of both the corpus's content and demographic metadata. Furthermore, it presents the current research being conducted with it —namely parenthetical expressions, orality traits, and code-switching. This work also includes a brief outline of similar corpora and recent studies in the field of IM, which shows the pertinence of the corpus and serves as a guideline for possible research.

1 Introduction

As digital communication technologies grow and spread, computer mediated communication (CMC) (Baron, 1984) —which includes (IM)— changes and becomes a very distinct sort of interaction. According to Álvarez (2011), a new discourse level emerges through such interaction —one that makes the distinction between writing and speaking less and less clear. This discourse style has been previously called both spoken writing (Blanco Rodríguez, 2002) and oralized text (Yus Ramos, 2010).

In order to study such a particular register, it is necessary to gather a robust corpus. The Sociolinguistic Corpus of WhatsApp Chats in Spanish for College Speech Analysis intends to be a resource that allows researchers to explore and characterize conversations held by college students and their peers, or other kind of participants, via the IM application known as WhatsApp (hereafter WA). This corpus is limited to bachelors studying at Ciudad Universitaria (commonly known as C.U.), the main campus of the National Autonomous University of Mexico (UNAM). The reason for choosing bachelors is because, in Mexico, 94.1% of the population with an undergraduate degree or a higher educational level uses the Internet for communication purposes, this mainly via IM, and generally they access the net on a smartphone. Furthermore, most of IM users are 12 to 34 years old, which is the age group the majority of college students belong to (INEGI, 2016).

2 State of the Art

2.1 Similar Corpora

Prior to the collection of WA corpora, other databases were created to allow the study of CMC. Examples of said data are the NPS Internet Chatroom Conversations Corpus (Forsyth et al., 2010), an annotated corpus of interactions in English in diverse chatrooms, and the Dortmunder Chat Corpus (Beisswenger, 2013), a robust, annotated corpus in German divided in 4 subcorpora, based on the topic of the chats (free time, learning contexts, cosultations, and media). In addition to these corpora, it is worth mentioning the NUS SMS Corpus (Chen and Kan, 2013) which comprises 71,000 messages, both in English and Chinese. Even though the SMS is not an internet-mediated mean of communication, it can be compared to interactions via WA.

Although the study of WA chats is a relatively novel research field, there are several corpora specialized mostly on them. One of the most impor-

1

Proceedings of the Sixth International Workshop on Natural Language Processing for Social Media , pages 1–6,
Melbourne, Australia, July 20, 2018. ©2018 Association for Computational Linguistics

tant projects is the one conducted by researchers of the Universities of Zurich, Bern, Neuchâtel and Leipzig. The *What's up, Switzerland?* corpus (Stark et al., 2014-) has as main aim the characterization of WA chats and the comparison of these to SMS. It has 617 chats written by 1,538 participants. Since just 945 of them consented to have their chats used, the total number of messages available for linguistic research is 763,650 comprising 5,543,692 tokens. Only 426 participants shared further demographic information (Überwasser and Stark, 2017). Given the fact that Switzerland is a multilingual country, 46% of the corpus is in German, 34% in French, 14% in Italian, 3% in Romansh and 3% in English. The sociodemographic information saved as metadata comprises age, gender, educational level, and place of residence divided in 9 regions. So far, the publications derived from this project focus not only on the different levels of language, but also the role of complementary items in conversation, such as images, acronyms, emojis, emoticons, and combination or modification of characters.

Verheijen and Stoop (2016) compiled a corpus which is a part of the SoNaR project (STEVIN *Nederlandstalig Referentiecorpus*) of posts and WA chats in Dutch. The corpus has 332,657 words in 15 chats donated by 34 informants. Their metadata encompasses informants' name, birth place and date, age, gende, educational level, and place in which the chats were sent. This corpus was used as one of the bases for a research where WA and other written forms were compared (Verheijen, 2017).

Hilte et al. (2017) compiled a corpus of chats between Flemish teenagers aged 13-20 taken from Facebook Messenger, WA, and iMessage. This, with the purpose of identifying the impact of social variables —namely age, gender and education— in teenagers' non-standard use of language in CMC.

In addition to these, an ongoing project is that of MoCoDa2 conducted by Beisswenger et al. (2017), which is a continuation of the preceeding corpus MoCoDa, and has put together 2,198 interactions with 19,161 user posts.

Nevertheless, all of these authors did not define what they conceive as a chat. In order to avoid any misconception, in the making of this corpus we consider a chat an exchange between two users regardless of length or date. Meaning that it does not matter when the conversation started, but rather the wholeness of the txt file.

Although there are, indeed, corpora of WA chats in Spanish, they are not for general use, but project-related. Besides, they are not as robust as the aforementioned. Said corpora are presented in the following section.

2.2 Research on WhatsApp Chats

Because of their peculiarities, virtual interactions through diverse platforms like WA, WeChat, Facebook Messenger, and so forth have drawn the attention of linguists. Some of the previous studies that have been conducted using similar corpora are varied in the topics they approach. Some of the aspects of language that can be studied with sociolinguistic corpora like ours are discourse units and phenomena such as turns and turntaking, speech acts, and interactions (Bani-Khair et al., 2016; Martín Gascueña, 2016; Alcántara Plá, 2014; García Arriola, 2014); linguistic variation from a diaphasic, diastratic or diatopic point of view (Pérez Sabater, 2015; Sánchez-Moya and Cruz-Moya, 2015); multimodal communication (verbal, iconic or hybrid) (Sánchez-Moya and Cruz-Moya, 2015); use of orthotypographic elements (Vázquez-Cano et al., 2015); the role of the so-called emojis in communication (Sampietro, 2016b,a; Dürscheid and Siever, 2017); and even the didactic use of IM for digital and linguistic competence (Gómez del Castillo, 2017).

Another phenomenon that has proved itself to be interesting is code-switching in IM (Nurhamidah, 2017; Zaehres, 2016; Zagoricnik, 2014). As Al-Emran and Al-Qaysi (2013) have stated "WhatsApp is found to be the most social networking App used for code-switching by both students and educators"; which is why authors like Elsayed (2014) have focused on such population.

3 Methodology

3.1 Sociolinguistic Variables in the Corpus

Considering this is a sociolinguistic corpus, several sociodemographic variables were defined as metadata and divided into two groups:

(a) Balance axes, which are the two variables that help to keep the balance and representativeness of the corpus:

- Sex: male or female [1]

---

[1] We chose sex over gender because it is the sociodemo-

- Faculty students are enrolled in: Architecture, Sciences, Political and Social Sciences, Accounting and Administration, Law, Economy, Philosophy and Literature, Engineering, Medicine, Veterinary Medicine, Odontology, Psychology, Chemistry, and the National School of Social Work.

Our goal was to collect at least 1% of the campus's population maintaining the same proportion of men and women as in each faculty.

(b) Post-stratification criteria, whose relevance will depend on the type of study conducted with this corpus as main data: age, (open answer), sexual orientation, (heterosexual, bisexual or homosexual), birthplace, (any state in Mexico), current place of residence, (post code), other languages, (any indigenous language spoken in Mexico or any language taught at UNAM), education level, (no formal education, elementary school, middle school, high school, bachelor's degree, master's degree, doctorate), major, (any undergraduate program offered at the Ciudad Universitaria campus), occupation, (student, working student, worker, unemployed or retired), profession (open answer), and kinship or type of relationship between speakers.

In overall, our corpus has 12 sociolinguistic variables that contribute to a large degree to the characterization and study of language in IM among youngsters. Furthermore, this allows our data to become a subcorpus of a much larger one in the future.

3.2 Data Collection

After establishing the sociodemographic metadata to be collected along with WA chats, the team proceeded to gather the data. In order to ease the data processing we collected chats with two participants only. All chats were donated as text files sent directly from the donors' devices, while metadata was collected manually. At the initial stage, the chats were collected using the directed sampling method. A team approached random students on campus explaining the project to them and inviting them to collaborate donating one or more WA chats. Those who consented to share

graphic variable used by UNAM in its statistics.

their chats -the donors- sent them via email to an institutional address, then were asked to answer a survey so the team could gather their and their interlocutor's sociodemographic information. After that, the information provided was entered into a spreadsheet along with a code that made it possible to link it to the corresponding text file. It is worth mentioning that the same metadata was collected with both methods.

3.3 Data Processing

The processing of data was done in two different stages. First, by means of a Python script, the collected data was saved into a spreadsheet. In the same stage, it was organized in JSON format and sent to the database as a document file. Second, a program allowed the users anonymity by changing their names in every chat to USER1 and USER2, and by deleting sensitive information —such as names, addresses, emails, phone numbers, bank accounts, and so forth.

Currently, queries can be done with both with Python scripts and MongoDB. Said tools permit the filtering of results depending on the metadata, allowing also the possibility of selecting relevant sociological variables and determining their ranges. In the future, we will develop an interface that makes the access and consultations to the database possible.

4 The Corpus

Although the corpus is still being processed, it has reached a mature stage which allows us to offer a general panorama of its content and demographics. The following figures represent the corpus state by March 2018. Should some changes be made, the final figures will be presented in future publications.

4.1 Content

Nowadays, we have 835 chats with 1,325 informants. After deleting dates, user names and all messages generated automatically by the app, we got 66,465 messages, 756,066 tokens and 45,497 types available for linguistic research.

Despite the fact that the vast majority of our informants are Mexican native Spanish speakers, texts in some other languages were found as well. Most of the messages in a language other than Spanish were written in English, however there are also texts in French, Japanese, Italian, German,

Korean, Greek and Chinese.

Other than that, we were also able to pinpoint which are the most frequently used lexical words among the informants. Students seem to be keen on using the ones displayed in Table 1.

Lexical Words		
bien	"good/well"	608,401
bueno	"good/well"	45,700
amor	"love"	44,900
bebé	"baby"	40,302
solo	"just/alone"	39,563

Table 1: Most frequent lexical words.

As it was previously mentioned, communication via IM shares several features with oral communication. However, since it lacks physical co-presence, it is necessary to develop some compensation strategies. Which is why emojis and emoticons are so widespread. The most frequent of these icons found in the corpus are shown in Table 2.

Emojis		Emoticons	
😂	2,221	xd	1,516
😭	1,015	:V	489
😆	445	:(	453
😊	435	:3	235
😌	249	:)	117

Table 2: Most frequent emojis and emoticons.

4.2 Demographics

As stated above, our corpus was built with the collaboration of 1,325 informants (51% women and 49% men), between ages 14 and 60, born in 23 of the 32 states in Mexico. Such a wide range of informants' age is due to the fact that some donors shared chats, held not with peers, but with people in their families, coworkers, or friends. Of all informants, 84.9% are undergraduates studying at C.U. Out of these students, 51.2% are women and 48.8% are men.

Henceforth, all figures refer only to bachelor informants. 80.7% of bachelors in the corpus were born in Mexico City, while 11.7% were born in Estado de México, the biggest state surrounding the capital. The rest were born in 20 other states —particularly Hidalgo, Guerrero and Michoacán.

Our corpus have also informants born in Chile (2), Colombia (1), The United States (1), and 3 that did not report their birthplace. 77.4% of our informants live in the city, while 19.4% live in Estado de México. The remaining 3.2% did not state their post code.

As to sexual orientation, 88.9% of students in the corpus declared themselves as heterosexual, 5.5 % bisexual and 5.4 % homosexual. Just .2% chose not to share such information.

Although the purpose of this corpus is to collect data from Mexican native Spanish speakers, some informants donated chats with people from other countries: Chile, Colombia, Costa Rica, Italy, Lebanon, and the United States, to name a few. All of these conversations were conducted mostly in Spanish. As second language, informants claimed to speak Arabian, Bulgarian, Chinese, English, French, German, modern Greek, Italian, Japanese, Korean, Nahuatl, Portuguese, Russian, or Swedish.

The students who donated their chats and their interlocutors belong to different faculties. The following table presents both the faculty roster at C.U. and the number of informants by sex.

Faculty	Male	Female	Total
Engineering	144	33	177
Accounting and Administration	71	52	123
Sciences	40	60	100
Political and Social Sciences	37	56	93
Chemistry	53	40	93
Philosophy and Literature	33	54	87
Medicine	27	50	77
Law	26	50	76
Architecture	32	42	74
Economy	39	22	61
Psychology	10	41	51
Veterinary Medicine	16	31	47
Odontology	15	25	40
National School of Social Work	7	20	27
Total	**550**	**576**	**1,126**

Table 3: Informants by faculty.

5   Current Research

At the time of the writing, there are three lines of research in the study of our corpus. One of them is parenthetical expressions that can work as repairs, instructions for interpretation, onomatopoetic expressions, surrogate prosodic cues to indicate how an utterance should be read, or surrogate proxemic cues such as emotes —sentences that indicate imaginary actions taking place at the moment of texting (Christopherson, 2010).

1. * se pone a llorar *
   "Starts crying."

2. (léase como si fuera eco)
   "Read as if it were an echo."

Another research line is the study of oral (phonic) traits in WA chats, for instance: the emulation of children's speech, repetition of vowels to indicate elongation of sounds, omission of letters to indicate consonant and vowel reduction, haplology, use of upper case for emphasis (volume), etc. (Yus Ramos, 2001)

3. kesestoooo
   Standard Spanish: ¿Qué es esto?
   "What is this?"

There is also the quantitative approach to code-switching from a sociolinguistic perspective, followed by a qualitative study of the forms and functions of it (Elsayed, 2014).

```
  Es que ya les urgía que te fueras.
: I know :(
  Jajaja, there there.
  Tomé mas whiskey de lo apropiado y no me puedo concentrar /:
: Is there even a thing as too much whiskey?
  You, my lady, are smart as fuck.
  Usualmente te diría que no.
  Pero tengo tarea :c
: It can help you get creative
:
```

Figure 1: Code-switching among bachelors.

6   Conclusion and Future Work

We presented a corpus that will make the study of language usage by college students via an Instant Messaging application possible. Its metadata will allow research, not only on mere linguistic phenomena, but also the stablishment of correlation between these and sociodemographic variables. Some of the phenomena that can be studied in interactions, such as the ones via IM, are phonic traits, parenthetical expressions, code-switching, turn-taking, speech acts, linguistic variation, and usage of emojis and emoticons.

Since the processing of data is still a work in progress. As next step, we plan to perform an evaluation of the anonymization process.

The objective of this corpus is to be used by both scholars and students in our group for the research of the aforementioned phenomena and others, and it is our intention to make it available upon request for others, with academic purposes only.

Acknowledgments

This work was supported by CONACYT project 002225 (2017) and CONACYT Redes 281795, as well as two DGAPA projects: IA400117 (2018) and IN403016 (2018).   We would also like to show our gratitude to students Ana Laura del Prado Mota, Mayra Paulina Díaz Rojas, and Paola Sánchez González for their participation in the collection and processing of data.

References

Mostafa Al-Emran and Noor Al-Qaysi. 2013. Code-switching usage in social media: A case study from oman. *International Journal of Information Technology and Language Studies(IJITLS)*, 1(1):25–38.

Manuel Alcántara Plá. 2014. Las unidades discursivas en los mensajes instantáneos de wasap. *Estudios de Lingüística del Español*, 35:223–242.

Baker Bani-Khair, Nisreen Al-Khawaldeh, Bassil Mashaqba, and Anas Huneety. 2016. A corpus-based discourse analysis study of whatsapp messenger's semantic notifications. *International Journal of Applied Linguistics & English Literature*, 5(6):158–165.

Naomi Baron. 1984. Computer-mediated communication as a force in language change. *Visible Language*, 18(2):118–141.

Michael Beisswenger. 2013. Das dortmunder chat-korpus. *Zeitschrift für germanistische Linguistik*.

Michael Beisswenger, Marcel Fladrich, Wolfgang Imo, and Evelyn Ziegler. 2017. Mocoda 2: Creating a database and web frontend for the repeated collection of mobile communication (whatsapp, sms & co.). In *Proceedings of the 5th Conference on CMC and Social Media Corpora for the Humanities (cmccorpora17)*, pages 11 – 15. Eurac Research.

Maria José Blanco Rodríguez. 2002. El chat: la conversación escrita. *ELUA. Estudios de Lingüística*, (16):43–87.

María-Teresa Gómez del Castillo. 2017. Whatsapp use for communication among graduates. *REICE. Revista Iberoamericana sobre Calidad, Eficacia y Cambio en Educación*, 15(4):51–65.

Tao Chen and Min-Yen Kan. 2013. Creating a live, public short message service corpus: the nus sms corpus. *Language Resources and Evaluation*, 47(2):299–335.

Laura Christopherson. 2010. What are people really saying in world of warcraft chat? In *Proceedings of the ASIST Annual Meeting*, volume 47. Learned Information.

Christa Dürscheid and Christina Siever. 2017. Beyond the alphabet – communication with emojis. pages 1–14.

Ahmed Samir Elsayed. 2014. Code switching in whatsapp messages among kuwaiti high school students.

Eric Forsyth, Jane Lin, and Craig Martell. 2010. Nps internet chatroom conversations, release 1.0 ldc2010t05.

Manuel García Arriola. 2014. Análisis de un corpus de conversaciones en whatsapp. aplicación del sistema de unidades conversacionales propuesto por el grupo val.es.co.

Lisa Hilte, Reinhild Vandekerckhove, and Walter Daelemans. 2017. Modeling non-standard language use in adolescents' cmc: The impact and interaction of age, gender and education. In *Proceedings of the 5th Conference on CMC and Social Media Corpora for the Humanities (cmccorpora17)*, page 71. Eurac Research.

INEGI. 2016. Encuesta nacional sobre disponibilidad y uso de tecnologías de la información en los hogares, 2016.

Rosa Martín Gascueña. 2016. La conversación guasap. *Sociocultural Pragmatics*, 4(1):108–134.

Idha Nurhamidah. 2017. Code-switching in whatsapp-exchanges: cultural or language barrier? In *Proceedings Education and Language International Conference*, pages 409–416. Center for International Language Development of Unissula.

Carmen Pérez Sabater. 2015. Discovering language variation in whatsapp text interactions. *Onomázein*, 31:113–126.

Agnese Sampietro. 2016a. *Emoticonos y emojis: Análisis de su historia, difusión y uso en la comunicación digital actual*. Ph.D. thesis, Universitat de València, La Coruña, Spain.

Agnese Sampietro. 2016b. Exploring the punctuating effect of emoji in spanish whatsapp chats. *Lenguas Modernas*, 47:91–113.

Elisabeth Stark, Simone Ueberwasser, and Anne Göhring. 2014-. Corpus "what's up, switzerland?".

Alfonso Sánchez-Moya and Olga Cruz-Moya. 2015. Whatsapp, textese, and moral panics: discourse features and habits across two generations. *Procedia - Social and Behavioral Sciences*, 173:300–206.

Lieke Verheijen. 2017. *WhatsApp with social media slang?: Youth language use in Dutch written computer-mediated communication*. Ljubljana University Press, Ljubljana, Slovenia.

Lieke Verheijen and Wessel Stoop. 2016. Collecting facebook posts and whatsapp chats: Corpus compilation of private social media messages. In *Lecture Notes in Computer Science (including subseries Lecture Notes in Artificial Intelligence and Lecture Notes in Bioinformatics)*, volume 9924, pages 249–258.

Esteban Vázquez-Cano, Andrés Santiago-Mengual, and Rosabel Roig-Vila. 2015. Análisis lexicométrico de la especificidad de la escritura digital del adolescente en whatsapp. *RLA. Revista de Lingüística Teórica y Aplicada*, 53(1):83–105.

Francisco Yus Ramos. 2001. *Ciberpragmática. El uso del lenguaje en Internet*. Ariel Lingüística. Ariel, Barcelona, Spain.

Francisco Yus Ramos. 2010. *Ciberpragmática 2.0: nuevos usos del lenguaje en Internet*. Ariel letras. Ariel, Barcelona, Spain.

Frederic Zaehres. 2016. A case study of code-switching in multilingual namibian keyboard-to-screen communication. *10plus1: Living Linguistics*.

Jelena Zagoricnik. 2014. Serbisch-schweizerdeutsches code-switsching in der whatsapp-kommunikation.

Isabel Álvarez. 2011. El ciberespañol: características del español usado en internet. In *Selected Proceedings of the 13th Hispanic Linguistics Symposium*, pages 1–11. Cascadilla Proceedings Project.

Simone Überwasser and Elisabeth Stark. 2017. What's up, switzerland? a corpus-based research project in a multilingual country. *Linguistik Online*, 84(5).

A Crowd-Annotated Spanish Corpus for Humor Analysis

Santiago Castro, Luis Chiruzzo, Aiala Rosá, Diego Garat, Guillermo Moncecchi
Grupo de Procesamiento de Lenguaje Natural
Facultad de Ingeniería
Universidad de la República — Uruguay
`{sacastro,luichir,aialar,dgarat,gmonce}@fing.edu.uy`

Abstract

Computational Humor involves several tasks, such as humor recognition, humor generation, and humor scoring, for which it is useful to have human-curated data. In this work we present a corpus of 27,000 tweets written in Spanish and crowd-annotated by their humor value and funniness score, with about four annotations per tweet, tagged by 1,300 people over the Internet. It is equally divided between tweets coming from humorous and non-humorous accounts. The inter-annotator agreement Krippendorff's alpha value is 0.5710. The dataset is available for general usage and can serve as a basis for humor detection and as a first step to tackle subjectivity.

1   Introduction

Computational Humor studies humor from a computational perspective, involving several tasks such as humor recognition, which aims to tell if a piece of text is humorous or not; humor generation, with the objective of generating new texts with funny content; and humor scoring, whose goal is to predict how funny a piece of text is.

In order to carry out this kind of tasks through supervised machine learning methods, human-curated data is necessary. Castro et al. (2016) built a humor classifier for Spanish and provided a dataset for humor recognition. However, there are some issues: few annotations per instance, low annotator agreement, and limited variety of sources for the humorous and mostly for the non-humorous tweets (the latter were only about news, inspirational thoughts and curious facts). Up to our knowledge, there is no other dataset to work on humor comprehension in Spanish. Some

other authors, such as Mihalcea and Strapparava (2005a,b); Sjöbergh and Araki (2007) have tackled humor recognition in English texts, building their own corpora by downloading *one-liners* (one-sentence jokes) from the Internet, since working with longer texts would involve additional work, such as determining humor scope.

The microblogging platform Twitter has been found particularly useful for building humor corpora due to its public availability and the fact that its short messages are suitable for jokes or humorous comments. Castro et al. (2016) built their corpus based on Twitter, selecting nine humorous accounts and nine non-humorous accounts about news, thoughts and curious facts. Reyes et al. (2013) built a corpus for detecting irony in tweets by searching for several hashtags (i.e., #irony, #humor, #education and #politics), which is also used in Barbieri and Saggion (2014) to train a classifier that detects humor. More recently, Potash et al. (2017) built a corpus based on tweets that aims to distinguish the degree of funniness in a given tweet. They used the tweet set issued in response to a TV game show, labeling which tweets were considered humorous by the show.

In this work we present a crowd-annotated Spanish corpus of tweets tagged with a humor/no humor value and also by a funniness score from one to five. The corpus contains tweets extracted from varied sources and has several annotations per tweet, reaching a high humor inter-annotator agreement.

The contribution of this work is twofold: the dataset is not only useful for building a humor classifier but it also serves to approach subjectivity in humor and funniness. Even though there are not enough annotations per tweet as required to study subjectivity in a genuine way with techniques such as the ones by Geng (2016), the dataset aids as a playground to study the funniness and disagree-

7

Proceedings of the Sixth International Workshop on Natural Language Processing for Social Media , pages 7–11,
Melbourne, Australia, July 20, 2018. ©2018 Association for Computational Linguistics

ment among several people.

This document is organized as follows. Section 2 explains where and how we obtained the data, and Section 3 describes how it was annotated. In Section 4 we present the corpus, and we address the analysis in Section 5. Finally, in Section 6 we present draw the conclusions and present the future work.

2 Extraction

The aim of the extraction and annotation process was to build a corpus of at least 20,000 tweets that was as balanced as possible between the humor and not humor classes. Furthermore, as we intended to have a way of calculating the funniness score of a tweet, we needed to have several votes for the tweets that were considered humorous.

As we wanted to have both humorous and non-humorous tweet samples, we extracted tweets from selected accounts and from realtime samples. For the former, based on Castro et al. (2016), we selected tweets from fifty humorous accounts from Spanish speaking countries, and took a random sample of size 12,000. For the latter, we fetched tweet samples written in Spanish throughout February 2018[1], and from this collection we took another random sample of size 12,000. Note that we preferred to take realtime tweet samples as we did not want to bias by selecting certain negative examples, such as news or inspirational thoughts as in Castro et al. (2016) and Mihalcea and Strapparava (2005b). From both sources we ignored retweets, responses, citations and tweets containing links, as we wanted the text to be self-contained. As expected, both sources contained a mix of humorous and non-humorous tweets. In the case of humorous accounts, this may be due to the fact that many tweets are used to increase the number of followers, expressing an opinion on a current event or supporting some popular cause.

We first aimed to have five votes for each tweet, and to decide which tweet was humorous by simple majority. However, at a certain stage during the annotation process, we noticed that the users were voting too many tweets as non-humorous, and the result was highly unbalanced. Because of this, we made some adjustments in the corpus and the process: as the target was to have five votes for each tweet, we considered that the

Figure 1: Example of a tweet presented to the annotators. It says: *I hate being bipolar, it's so cool!*. The annotator is asked whether the tweet intends to be humorous. The available options are "Yes", "No" or "Skip". If the annotator selects "Yes", five emoji are shown so the annotator can specify how funny he considers the tweet. The emoji also include labels describing the funniness levels.

tweets that already had three non-humorous annotations at this stage should be considered as not humor, then we deprioritized them so the users could focus in annotating the rest of the tweets that were still ambiguous. We also injected 4,500 more tweets randomly extracted only from the humorous accounts. These new tweets were also prioritized since they had less annotations than the rest.

3 Annotation

A crowdsourced web annotation task was carried out to tag all tweets.[2] The annotators were shown tweets as in Fig. 1. The tweets were randomly chosen but web session information was kept to avoid showing duplicates. We tried to keep the user interface as intuitive and self-explanatory as possible, trying not to induce any bias on users and letting them come up with their own definition of humor. The simple and friendly interface is meant to keep the users engaged and having fun while classifying tweets as humorous or not, and how funny they are, with as few instructions as possible.

If a person decides that a tweet is humorous, he has to rate it between one to five by using emoji. In this way, the annotator gives more information rather than just stating the tweet is humorous. We also allowed to skip a tweet or click a help button for more information. We consider that explicitly asking the annotator if the text intends to be humorous makes the distinction between the Not Humorous and Not Funny classes less ambiguous,

---

[1]The language detection feature is provided by the Twitter REST API.

[2]https://clasificahumor.com

which we believe was a problem of (Castro et al., 2016) user interface. Also, we consider our emoji rated funniness score to be clearer for annotators than their stars based rating.

The web page was shared on popular social networks along with some context about the task and the annotation period occurred between March 8th and 27th, 2018. The first tweets shown to every session were the same: three tweets for which we know a clear answer (one of them was humorous and the other two were not). These first tweets ("test tweets") were meant as a way of introducing the user into how the interface works, and also as an initial way for evaluating the quality of the annotations. After the introductory tweets, the rest of the tweets were sampled randomly, starting with the ones with the least number of votes.

4 Corpus

The dataset consists of two CSV files: tweets and annotations. The former contains the identifier and origin (which can be the realtime samples or the selected accounts) for each one of the $27,282$ tweets[3], while the latter contains the tweet identifier, session identifier, date and annotation value for each one of the $117,800$ annotations received during the annotation phase (including the times the skip button was pressed, $2,959$ times). The dataset was released and it is available online.[4]

When compiling the final version of the corpus, we considered the annotations of users that did not answer the first three tweets correctly as having lower quality. These sessions should not be used for training or testing machine learning algorithms. Fortunately, only a small number of annotations had to be discarded because of this reason. The final number of annotations is $107,634$ (not including the times the skip button was pressed), including $3,916$ annotations assigned to the test tweets themselves.

5 Analysis

5.1 Annotation Distribution

Each tweet received 3.8 annotations on average, with a standard deviation of 1.16, not considering the test tweets as they are outliers (they have a large number of annotations). The annotation

---

[3]Tweet text is not included in the corpus due to Twitter Terms and Conditions. They can be obtained from the IDs.
[4]https://pln-fing-udelar.github.io/humor

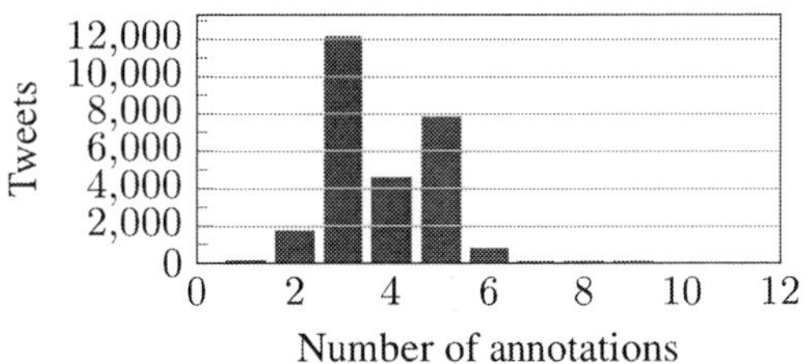

Figure 2: Distribution of tweets by number of annotations. Most tweets have between two and six annotations each.

distribution is shown in Fig. 2. The histogram is highly concentrated: more than 98% of the tweets received between two and six annotations each. Even though the strategy was to show random tweets among the ones with less annotations, note that there are tweets with less than three annotations because some annotations were finally filtered out. At the same time, there are some tweets with more than six annotations because we merged annotations from a few dozen duplicate tweets. Also, note that there is a considerable amount of tweets with at least six annotations $(1,001)$. This subset can be useful to study the different annotator opinions under the same instances.

5.2 Class Distribution

Fig. 3 shows how the classes are distributed between the annotations. Roughly two thirds were assigned to the class Not Humorous, agreeing with the fact that there seem to be more non-humorous tweets from humorous accounts than the other way around. The graph also indicates that there is a bias towards bad jokes in humor, according to the annotators. We use simple majority of votes for categorizing between humorous or not humorous, and weighted average for computing the funniness score only for humorous tweets. The scale goes from one (Not Funny) to five (Excellent). Under this scheme, 27.01% of the tweets are humorous, 70.6% are not-humorous while 2.39% is undecided (2.38% tied and 0.01% no annotations). At the same time, humorous tweets have little funniness overall: the funniness score average is 1.35 and standard deviation 0.85.

5.3 Annotators Distribution

There were $1,271$ annotators who tagged the tweets roughly as follows: two annotators tagged $13,000$ tweets, then one annotated $8,000$, the next eight annotated between one and three thousand,

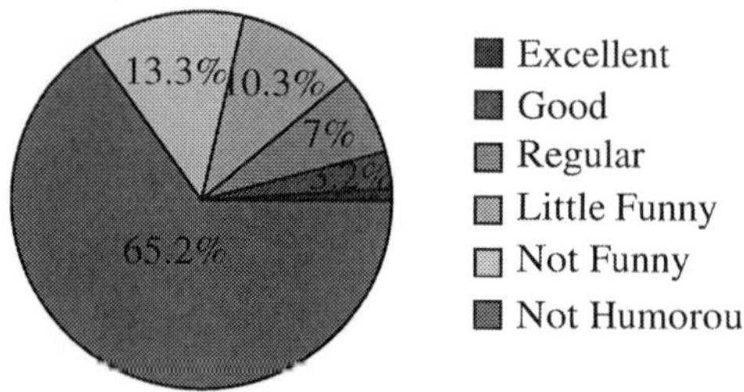

Figure 3: Annotations according to their class.

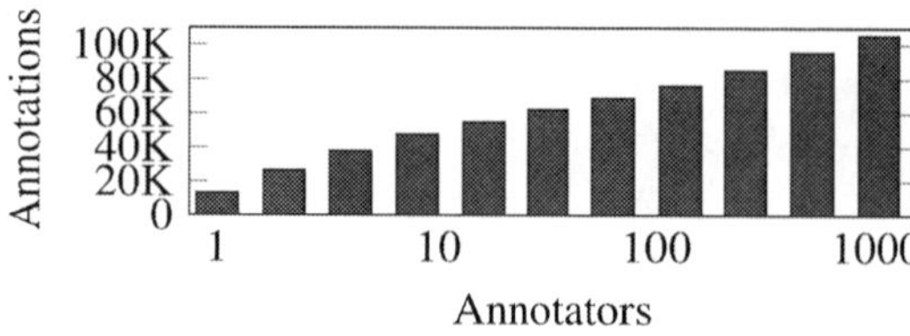

Figure 4: Accumulated distribution of annotations by number of annotators. Notice that the top 100 annotators add up to more than $70,000$ annotations.

the next 105 annotated between one hundred and one thousand and the rest annotated less than a hundred, having $32,584$ annotations in total (see Fig. 4). The average was 83 tags by annotator, with a standard deviation of 597.

5.4 Annotators Agreement

An important aspect to analyze is to what extent the annotators agree on which tweets are humorous. We used the *alpha* measure from Krippendorff (2012), a generalized version of the *kappa* measure (Cohen, 1960; Fleiss, 1971) that takes in account an arbitray number of raters. The agreement alpha value on humorous versus non-humorous is 0.5710. According to Fleiss (1981), it means that the agreement is somewhat between "moderate" to "substantial", suggesting there is acceptable agreement but the humans cannot completely agree. We believe that the carefully designed user interface impacted in the quality of the annotation, as unlike Castro et al. (2016) this work's annotation web page presented less ambiguity between the class Not Humorous and Not Funny. We clearly outperformed their inter-annotator agreement (which was 0.3654). Additionally, if we consider the whole corpus (including the removed annotations), this figure decreases to 0.5512. This shows that the test tweets were helpful to filter out low quality annotations.

Additionally, we can try to estimate to what extent the annotators agree on the funniness value of the tweets. In this case, disagreement between close values in the scale (e.g. Not Funny and Little Funny) should have less impact than disagreement between values that are further (e.g. Not Funny and Excellent). Following Stevens (1946), in the previous case we were dealing with a *nominal* measure while in this case it is an *ordinal* measure. Alpha considers this into the formula by using a generic distance function between ratings, so we applied it and obtained a value of 0.1625 which is far from good; it is closer to a random annotation. There is a lack of agreement on the funniness. In this case, a machine will not be able to assign a unique value of funniness to a tweet, which makes sense with its subjectivity, albeit other techniques could be used (Geng, 2016). In this case, if we consider the whole dataset, this number decreases to 0.1442.

If we only consider the eleven annotators who tagged more than a thousand times (who tagged $50,939$ times in total), the humor and funniness agreement are respectively 0.6345 and 0.2635.

6 Conclusion and Future Work

Our main contribution is a corpus of tweets in Spanish labeled by their humor value and funniness score with respect to a crowd-sourced annotation. The dataset contains $27,282$ tweets coming from multiple sources, with $107,634$ annotations. The corpus showed high quality because of the significant inter-annotator agreement value.

The dataset serves to build a Spanish humor classifier, but it also serves as a first step to tackle humor and funniness subjectivity. Even though more annotations per tweet would be appropriate, there is a subset of a thousand tweets with at least six annotations that could be used to study people's opinion on the same instances.

Future steps involve gathering more annotations per tweet for a considerable amount of tweets, so techniques such as the ones in (Geng, 2016) could be used to study how people perceive the humorous pieces and what subjects and phrases they consider funnier. It would be interesting to consider social strata (e.g. origin, age and gender) when trying to find these patterns. Additionally, a similar dataset could be built for other languages which count with more data to cross over with (such as English) and build a humor classifier exploiting recent Deep Learning techniques based on it.

Acknowledgments

We thank everyone who annotated tweets via the web page. We would not have been able to reach the large number of annotations we have got without their help.

References

Francesco Barbieri and Horacio Saggion. 2014. Automatic detection of irony and humour in twitter. In *ICCC*, pages 155–162.

Santiago Castro, Matías Cubero, Diego Garat, and Guillermo Moncecchi. 2016. Is this a joke? detecting humor in spanish tweets. In *Ibero-American Conference on Artificial Intelligence*, pages 139–150. Springer.

Jacob Cohen. 1960. A coefficient of agreement for nominal scales. *Educational and psychological measurement*, 20(1):37–46.

Joseph L Fleiss. 1971. Measuring nominal scale agreement among many raters. *Psychological bulletin*, 76(5):378.

Joseph L Fleiss. 1981. *Statistical methods for rates and proportions*, 2 edition. John Wiley.

Xin Geng. 2016. Label distribution learning. *IEEE Transactions on Knowledge and Data Engineering*, 28(7):1734–1748.

Klaus Krippendorff. 2012. *Content analysis: An introduction to its methodology*. Sage.

Rada Mihalcea and Carlo Strapparava. 2005a. Bootstrapping for fun: Web-based construction of large data sets for humor recognition. In *Proceedings of the Workshop on Negotiation, Behaviour and Language (FINEXIN 2005)*, volume 3814, pages 84–93.

Rada Mihalcea and Carlo Strapparava. 2005b. Making computers laugh: Investigations in automatic humor recognition. In *Proceedings of the Conference on Human Language Technology and Empirical Methods in Natural Language Processing*, HLT '05, pages 531–538, Stroudsburg, PA, USA. Association for Computational Linguistics.

Peter Potash, Alexey Romanov, and Anna Rumshisky. 2017. Semeval-2017 task 6:# hashtagwars: Learning a sense of humor. In *Proceedings of the 11th International Workshop on Semantic Evaluation (SemEval-2017)*, pages 49–57.

Antonio Reyes, Paolo Rosso, and Tony Veale. 2013. A multidimensional approach for detecting irony in twitter. *Language resources and evaluation*, 47(1):239–268.

Jonas Sjöbergh and Kenji Araki. 2007. Recognizing humor without recognizing meaning. In *WILF*, volume 4578 of *Lecture Notes in Computer Science*, pages 469–476. Springer.

Stanley Smith Stevens. 1946. On the theory of scales of measurement. *Science*, 103:677–680.

A Twitter Corpus for Hindi-English Code Mixed POS Tagging

Kushagra Singh
IIIT Delhi

Indira Sen
IIIT Delhi

Ponnurangam Kumaraguru
IIIT Delhi

`{kushagra14056,indira15021,pk}@iiitd.ac.in`

Abstract

Code-mixing is a linguistic phenomenon where multiple languages are used in the same occurrence that is increasingly common in multilingual societies. Code-mixed content on social media is also on the rise, prompting the need for tools to automatically understand such content. Automatic Parts-of-Speech (POS) tagging is an essential step in any Natural Language Processing (NLP) pipeline, but there is a lack of annotated data to train such models. In this work, we present a unique language tagged and POS-tagged dataset of code-mixed English-Hindi tweets related to five incidents in India that led to a lot of Twitter activity. Our dataset is unique in two dimensions: **(i)** it is larger than previous annotated datasets and **(ii)** it closely resembles typical real-world tweets. Additionally, we present a POS tagging model that is trained on this dataset to provide an example of how this dataset can be used. The model also shows the efficacy of our dataset in enabling the creation of code-mixed social media POS taggers.

1 Introduction

With the rise of Web 2.0, the volume of text on Online Social Networks (OSN) has grown. Bilingual or trilingual social media users have thus contributed to a multilingual corpus containing a combination of formal and informal posts. Code-switching or code-mixing[1] occurs when "lexical items and grammatical features from two languages appear in one sentence" (Muysken, 2000).

It is frequently seen in multilingual communities and is of interest to linguists due to its complex relationship with societal factors. Past research has looked at multiple dimensions of this behaviour, such as it's relationship to emotion expression (Rudra et al., 2016) and identity. But research efforts are often hindered by the lack of automated Natural Language Processing (NLP) tools to analyze massive amounts of code-mixed data (Bali et al., 2014). POS tags are used as features for downstream NLP tasks and past research has investigated how to obtain accurate POS tags for noisy OSN data. POS tagging for Code-mixed social media data has also been investigated (Gimpel et al., 2011), however, existing datasets are either hard to obtain or lacking in comprehensiveness.

In this work, we present a language and POS-tagged Hindi-English (Hi-En from now on) dataset of 1,489 tweets (33,010 tokens) that closely resembles the topical mode of communication on Twitter. Our dataset is more extensive than any existing code-mixed POS tagged dataset and is rich in Twitter specific tokens such as hashtags and mentions, as well as topical and situational information. We make the entire dataset and our POS tagging model available publicly[2].

2 Related Work

POS tagging is an important stage of an NLP pipeline (Cutting et al., 1992) and has been explored extensively (Toutanova et al., 2003a; Gimpel et al., 2011; Owoputi et al., 2013). However, these models perform poorly on textual content generated on OSNs, including and specially tweets (Ritter et al., 2011). This is due to subtle variations in text generated on OSNs from written and spoken text, such as slack grammatical structure, spelling variations and ad-hoc abbrevi-

---

[1]Both the terms "code-mixing" and "code-switching" are used interchangeably by many researchers

[2]http://precog.iiitd.edu.in/resources.html

12

Proceedings of the Sixth International Workshop on Natural Language Processing for Social Media , pages 12–17,
Melbourne, Australia, July 20, 2018. ©2018 Association for Computational Linguistics

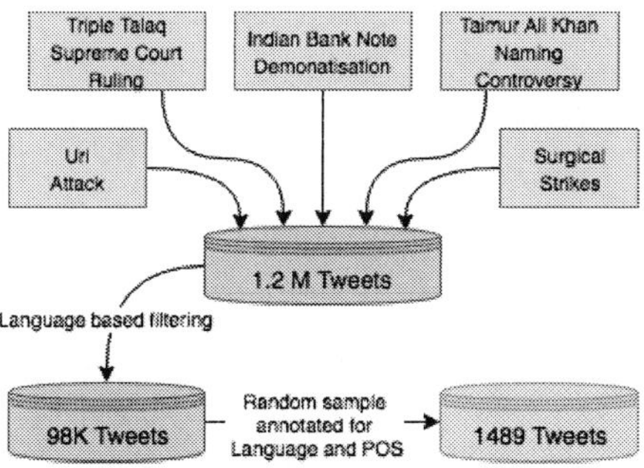

Figure 1: The dataset creation pipeline.

ations. An elaborate discussion on the differences between tweets and traditional textual content has been done by Ritter et al. (2011).

In addition to the variations between OSN and traditional textual content, code-mixing adds another layer of difficulty (Bali et al., 2014). To bypass these differences, POS taggers have been trained on Hi-En code-mixed posts generated on Facebook (Vyas et al., 2014; Sharma et al., 2016), however, the datasets used for training the models are not available for further experimentation and benchmarking. Only one public dataset of En-Hi code-mixed Twitter posts annotated for POS tags exists (Jamatia and Das, 2016), which comprises of 1,096 tweets (17,311 tokens)[3]. The dataset proposed in this paper is Twitter specific, larger than existing datasets (1,489 tweets, 33,010 tokens) and is event-driven.

3 Dataset Creation

In this section we discuss our data collection methodology and our annotation process. Our data comprises of tweets related to five events, which are (i) the attack by insurgents in the Uri region of Kashmir, India[4], (ii) the Supreme Court ruling that declared Triple Talaq unconstitutional[5], (iii) the Indian banknote demonetization[6], (iv) the Taimur Ali Khan name controversy[7] and (v) the surgical strike carried out by the Indian Army in Pakistan.[8]

---

[3]This dataset also comprises of 772 Facebook posts and 762 WhatsApp messages

[4]https://reut.rs/2HhBQPg

[5]https://reut.rs/2JDecet

[6]https://reut.rs/2GVKEep

[7]https://bbc.in/2IMPd6Y

[8]https://reut.rs/2EHQZ7g

3.1 Data Collection and Selection

We first select a set of candidate hashtags related to the five incidents. Using Twitter's streaming API, we collect tweets which contain at least one of these hashtags. For each incident, we collect tweets over a period of 14 days from the day of the incident, collecting 1,210,543 tweets in all.

Previous work has noted that code mixed content forms a fraction of tweets generated, even in multilingual societies (Rudra et al., 2016). To have a high proportion of code mixed tweets in our dataset, we run the language identification model by Sharma et al. (2016) on the tweets and select those which meet all of the following criterion : (i) contains least three Hindi tokens, (ii) contains at least three English tokens, (iii) contains at least 2 contiguous Hindi tokens and (iv) contains at least 2 contiguous English tokens. After this filtering, we are left with 98,867 tweets.

We manually inspect 100 randomly sampled tweets and find that many named entities (NEs) such as 'Kashmir', 'Taimur' and 'Modi' are identified as Hindi. Since manual correction of so many tweets would be difficult, and the problem of misidentifying the language tag of NEs would persist in real life, we include these in our dataset. This misclassification explains the presence of English tweets in our dataset. From the filtered set, we randomly sample 1500 tweets for manual annotation of language and POS. Some of these tweets contain a high number of foreign words (not belonging to English or Hindi). We manually remove such tweets during the annotation process. We maintain the structure of the tweet as it is, and do not split it into multiple sentences. Finally, we tokenize the tweets using twokenizer (Owoputi et al., 2013), which yields 33010 tokens in all.

3.2 Data Annotation

Two bilingual speakers fluent in English and Hindi (one of whom is a linguist) annotate each tweet at the token level for its language and POS. The tags generated by the Language Identifier used for filtering earlier are stripped off. We find that the Language Identifier correctly labeled 82.1% of the tokens, with most misclassification being due to NEs. We note that misclassifications also occur at the boundaries between the Hindi and English part of tweets.

```
TOKEN           LANG  POS
Lets            en    VERB
take            en    VERB
Pakistan        rest  PROPN
under           en    ADP
our             en    PRON
control         en    NOUN
.               rest  X
Na              hi    PART_NEG
rahega          hi    VERB
bass            hi    NOUN
na              hi    PART_NEG
rahegi          hi    VERB
basuri          hi    NOUN
.               rest  X
#Uriattack      rest  X
#Pakistan       rest  X
#India          rest  X
@PMOIndia       rest  X
@rajnathsingh   rest  X
@arunjaitley    rest  X
```

Figure 2: A randomly selected code-mixed tweet from our dataset. The three columns represent the original token, the language tag and the POS tag.

3.2.1 Language Annotation

We use annotation guidelines followed by Bali et al. (2014). Each token is assigned either *hi*, *en* or *rest*. All NEs, Twitter specific tokens (Hashtags and Mentions), acronyms, symbols, words not belonging to Hindi or English, and sub-lexically code-mixed tokens are marked as *rest*. Table 1 and 2 describe the language distribution of our data on a tweet level and token level respectively. Language annotation has a high inter-annotator agreement of 0.97 (Cohen's κ).

3.2.2 Part Of Speech Annotation

Since we look at two different languages, we follow the universal POS set proposed by Petrov et al. (2011) which attempts to cover POS tags across all languages. We reproduce the universal POS set with some alterations, which are (i) We use **PROPN** to annotate proper nouns. We do this to enable further research with this dataset by exploring named entity recognition (NER) which benefits from explicitly labeled proper nouns. All other nouns are tagged as NOUN. (ii) We use **PART_NEG** to annotate Negative Particles. PART_NEG aids in sentiment detection where the presence of a negation word denotes the flipping of sentiment. All other particles are tagged as PART. (iii) We use **PRON_WH** to annotate interrogative pronouns (like where, why, etc.) This shall help in building systems for question detection, another important NLP task. All other pronouns are tagged as PRON.

In the universal set **X** is used to denote for-

Language	Tweets
Code-mixed	1077 (72.33 %)
English	343 (23.04 %)
Hindi	69 (4.63 %)
Total	1489

Table 1: Language distribution of tweets. Presence of monolingual tweets is due to errors in the output of the language detection model.

Language	All Tweets	Code-mixed Tweets
English	12589 (38.14 %)	7954 (32.64)
Hindi	9882 (29.94 %)	9093 (37.31)
Rest	10539 (31.93 %)	7323 (30.05)
Total	33010	24370

Table 2: Language distribution of tokens. We observe a fairly balanced spread across the classes.

eign words, typos, abbreviations. We also include punctuation under this category. Additionally Twitter-specific tokens hashtags and mentions are also included under X. While (Gimpel et al., 2011) use finer categories for Twitter-specific tokens, we neglect to do so since these tokens can be detected using rule-based features and would artificially boost a POS tagger's accuracy. Figure 2 provides an example of a tweet, and it's corresponding language and POS tag annotation. Inter-annotator agreement for POS tagging was 0.88 (Cohen's κ), all differences were resolved through discussion.

3.3 Data Statistics

Table 3 summarizes the distribution of POS tags in our dataset. We see that there is indeed a high fraction of NEs and that on average, there are 1.84 NEs per tweet. The presence of NEs is confirmed in previous research that event-driven Twitter activity has significant NE content (De Choudhury et al., 2012). We also see a significant amount (421 occurrences) of interrogative pronouns, which in conjunction with 258 occurrences of the '?' symbol signals the presences of inquiries.

4 Experiments

In this section, we demonstrate how our POS-tagged dataset can be used, by building and evaluating an automatic POS tagging model. We present a set of hand-crafted features using which

POS	All tweets	Code Mixed tweets
NOUN	5043 (14.618 %)	3844 (15.773 %)
PROPN	2737 (7.934 %)	1634 (6.705 %)
VERB	5984 (17.346 %)	4566 (18.736 %)
ADJ	1548 (4.487 %)	1116 (4.579 %)
ADV	1021 (2.96 %)	816 (3.348 %)
DET	1141 (3.307 %)	778 (3.192 %)
ADP	2982 (8.644 %)	2229 (9.146 %)
PRON	1456 (4.221 %)	1095 (4.493 %)
PRON_WH	421 (1.22 %)	325 (1.334 %)
PART	1428 (4.139 %)	1122 (4.604 %)
PART_NEG	468 (1.357 %)	399 (1.637 %)
NUM	391 (1.133 %)	309 (1.268 %)
CONJ	809 (2.345 %)	564 (2.314 %)
X	7581 (21.975 %)	5573 (22.868 %)
Total	33010	24370

Table 3: Class wise Part of Speech tag distribution in all Tweets and Code Mixed tweets

POS	POS_{base}	POS_{base+}	POS_{CRF}	POS_{LSTM}
NOUN	72.37	75.95	84.08	72.23
PROPN	81.58	81.68	92.22	80.51
VERB	82.97	79.48	87.84	80.72
ADJ	70.68	69.94	74.92	64.66
ADV	79.26	79.89	82.47	65.92
DET	93.00	95.22	90.50	88.69
ADP	92.92	94.14	93.75	83.75
PRON	87.57	90.91	89.22	83.75
PRON_WH	92.81	93.51	95.60	92.72
PART	78.04	79.93	78.37	73.23
PART_NEG	98.27	98.27	98.27	97.14
NUM	87.32	87.32	90.54	85.51
CONJ	93.55	93.81	93.59	89.23
X	76.11	94.86	98.80	94.51
Total	80.77	85.64	**90.20**	82.51

Table 4: Class wise F_1 score (percentage) of different models on the validation set.

our models learn to predict the POS tag of a token. We compare the performance of our models with two naive baselines, POS_{base} and POS_{base+}. POS_{base} assigns the most frequent POS tag to a token, as seen in the training data. POS_{base+} also does the same, but considers the language of the token as well.

For our experiments, we hold out 20% of the data as a validation set. We perform five-fold cross-validation on the remaining 80% for parameter tuning, and report the performance of our models on the validation set in Table 4.

4.1 Model and Features

We attempt to model POS tagging as a sequence labeling task using Conditional Random Field (CRF) and LSTM Recurrent Neural Networks. Previous research has validated the use of CRFs (Toutanova et al., 2003b; Choi et al., 2005; Peng and McCallum, 2006) and LSTM RNNs (Ghosh et al., 2016; Wang et al., 2015) for POS tagging and other sequence labeling NLP tasks.

Our LSTM model has two recurrent layers comprising of 32 bidirectional LSTM cells each. The output of the second layer at each timestep is connected to a softmax layer, used to perform classification over the set of POS tags. Our CRF model is a standard CRF model as proposed by (Lafferty et al., 2001).

We use the following as features for our classifier : **(i)** The current token T, T after stripping all characters which are not in the Roman alphabet (T_{clean}), and converting all characters in T_{clean} to lowercase (T_{norm}) generates three different features, **(ii)** the language tag of T, **(iii)** length of T, **(iv)** Fraction of ASCII characters in T, **(v)** affixes of length 1 to 3, padded with whitespace if needed, **(vi)** a binary feature indicating whether T is titlecased, **(vii)** a binary feature indicating whether T has any upper case character, **(viii)** a binary feature indicating whether there is a non alphabetic character in T and **(ix)** a binary feature indicating whether all characters in T are uppercase.

To prevent overfitting we add a dropout of 0.5 after every layer (for the LSTM model), and L_1 and L_2 regularization (both models). We perform grid search with 5-fold cross validation to find the optimal values for these parameters.

We supplement the models with a list of rules to detect Twitter specific tokens (such as Hashtags, Mentions, etc.) and Numerals. We follow an approach along the lines of (Ritter et al., 2011) and use regular expressions to make a set of rules for detecting such tokens. Since these are trivial to detect, we omit these tokens while evaluating the performance of the model.

4.2 Results and Error Analysis

Our best model is POS_{CRF}, which achieves an overall F_1 score of 90.20% (Table 4). Using the same feature set without language tags led to a slight decrease in F_1 score (88.64%). Decrease in POS tagging performance due to language tags is corroborated in previous literature (Vyas et al., 2014). The POS_{LSTM} model performs poorly (F_1 score of 82.51%). We notice that despite using regularization, the model starts overfitting very quickly.

The performance of our POS tagging models across all POS tag categories is shown in Table 4. We find that our POS tagger performs poorest in detecting Hindi adjectives since Hindi has a more relaxed grammatical structure where an adjective may precede as well as follow a noun, e.g.

Tweet: "U people only talk..no action will be taken! *Aap log darpok ho kewal* Twitter ke sher ho. #UriAttack"

Gloss: "you people only talk..no action will be taken! *you (aap) people (log) timid(darpok) are(ho)* only(kewal) Twitter of(ke) tiger(sher) are(ho). #UriAttack"

Translation: "you people only talk..no action will be taken! *you people are timid*, only tiger of Twitter. #UriAttack"

In the above tweet, the adjective 'timid' follows the noun 'people' instead of the usual format seen in English. A similar trend is observed in adverbs.

5 Discussion

In this data paper, we present a unique dataset curated from Twitter regarding five popular incidents. This dataset differs from previous POS tagged resources both regarding size and lexical structure. We believe that our dataset aids in building effective POS-tagger in order to capture the nuances of Twitter conversation.

We note that our model suffers lower performance for POS tag categories like adjectives and adverbs which follow a different set of grammatical rules for Hindi versus English. In future, we would like to have two POS taggers for differently structured grammar sets and combine them. We also find that our model can detect NEs which is essential when analyzing event-driven tweets. Our dataset therefore also facilitates further research in Named Entity Recognition. We also note the significant amount of interrogative pronouns in our dataset. This suggests that events generate inquiries and questions in the mind of Twitter users.

In future, we would also like to explore building other downstream NLP tools such as Parsers or Sentiment Analyzers which make use of POS tags using our dataset and refined versions of our POS tagging model.

References

Kalika Bali, Jatin Sharma, Monojit Choudhury, and Yogarshi Vyas. 2014. "i am borrowing ya mixing ?" an analysis of english-hindi code mixing in facebook. In *Proceedings of the First Workshop on Computational Approaches to Code Switching*. Association for Computational Linguistics, pages 116–126. https://doi.org/10.3115/v1/W14-3914.

Yejin Choi, Claire Cardie, Ellen Riloff, and Siddharth Patwardhan. 2005. Identifying sources of opinions with conditional random fields and extraction patterns. In *Proceedings of the conference on Human Language Technology and Empirical Methods in Natural Language Processing*. Association for Computational Linguistics, pages 355–362.

Doug Cutting, Julian Kupiec, Jan Pedersen, and Penelope Sibun. 1992. A practical part-of-speech tagger. In *Proceedings of the third conference on Applied natural language processing*. Association for Computational Linguistics, pages 133–140.

Munmun De Choudhury, Nicholas Diakopoulos, and Mor Naaman. 2012. Unfolding the event landscape on twitter: classification and exploration of user categories. In *Proceedings of the ACM 2012 conference on Computer Supported Cooperative Work*. ACM, pages 241–244.

Shalini Ghosh, Oriol Vinyals, Brian Strope, Scott Roy, Tom Dean, and Larry Heck. 2016. Contextual lstm (clstm) models for large scale nlp tasks. *arXiv preprint arXiv:1602.06291* .

Kevin Gimpel, Nathan Schneider, Brendan O'Connor, Dipanjan Das, Daniel Mills, Jacob Eisenstein, Michael Heilman, Dani Yogatama, Jeffrey Flanigan, and Noah A Smith. 2011. Part-of-speech tagging for twitter: Annotation, features, and experiments. In *Proceedings of the 49th Annual Meeting of the Association for Computational Linguistics: Human Language Technologies: short papers-Volume 2*. Association for Computational Linguistics, pages 42–47.

Anupam Jamatia and Amitava Das. 2016. Task report: Tool contest on pos tagging for code-mixed indian social media (facebook, twitter, and whatsapp) text @ icon 2016. In *Proceedings of ICON 2016*.

John D. Lafferty, Andrew McCallum, and Fernando C. N. Pereira. 2001. Conditional random fields: Probabilistic models for segmenting and labeling sequence data. In *Proceedings of the Eighteenth International Conference on Machine Learning*. Morgan Kaufmann Publishers Inc., San Francisco, CA, USA, ICML '01, pages 282–289. http://dl.acm.org/citation.cfm?id=645530.655813.

Pieter Muysken. 2000. *Bilingual speech: A typology of code-mixing*, volume 11. Cambridge University Press.

Olutobi Owoputi, Brendan O'Connor, Chris Dyer, Kevin Gimpel, Nathan Schneider, and Noah A Smith. 2013. Improved part-of-speech tagging for online conversational text with word clusters. Association for Computational Linguistics.

Fuchun Peng and Andrew McCallum. 2006. Information extraction from research papers using conditional random fields. *Information processing & management* 42(4):963–979.

Slav Petrov, Dipanjan Das, and Ryan McDonald. 2011. A universal part-of-speech tagset. *arXiv preprint arXiv:1104.2086* .

Alan Ritter, Sam Clark, Oren Etzioni, et al. 2011. Named entity recognition in tweets: an experimental study. In *Proceedings of the Conference on Empirical Methods in Natural Language Processing*. Association for Computational Linguistics, pages 1524–1534.

Koustav Rudra, Shruti Rijhwani, Rafiya Begum, Kalika Bali, Monojit Choudhury, and Niloy Ganguly. 2016. Understanding language preference for expression of opinion and sentiment: What do hindi-english speakers do on twitter? In *EMNLP*. pages 1131–1141.

Arnav Sharma, Sakshi Gupta, Raveesh Motlani, Piyush Bansal, Manish Shrivastava, Radhika Mamidi, and Dipti M Sharma. 2016. Shallow parsing pipeline for hindi-english code-mixed social media text. In *Proceedings of NAACL-HLT*. pages 1340–1345.

Kristina Toutanova, Dan Klein, Christopher D. Manning, and Yoram Singer. 2003a. Feature-rich part-of-speech tagging with a cyclic dependency network. In *Proceedings of the 2003 Conference of the North American Chapter of the Association for Computational Linguistics on Human Language Technology - Volume 1*. Association for Computational Linguistics, Stroudsburg, PA, USA, NAACL '03, pages 173–180. https://doi.org/10.3115/1073445.1073478.

Kristina Toutanova, Dan Klein, Christopher D Manning, and Yoram Singer. 2003b. Feature-rich part-of-speech tagging with a cyclic dependency network. In *Proceedings of the 2003 Conference of the North American Chapter of the Association for Computational Linguistics on Human Language Technology-Volume 1*. Association for Computational Linguistics, pages 173–180.

Yogarshi Vyas, Spandana Gella, Jatin Sharma, Kalika Bali, and Monojit Choudhury. 2014. Pos tagging of english-hindi code-mixed social media content. In *EMNLP*. volume 14, pages 974–979.

Peilu Wang, Yao Qian, Frank K Soong, Lei He, and Hai Zhao. 2015. A unified tagging solution: Bidirectional lstm recurrent neural network with word embedding. *arXiv preprint arXiv:1511.00215* .

Detecting Offensive Tweets in Hindi-English Code-Switched Language

Puneet Mathur
Netaji Subhas Institute of Technology
Delhi, India
pmathur3k6@gmail.com

Rajiv Ratn Shah
IIIT-Delhi
Delhi, India
rajivratn@iiitd.ac.in

Ramit Sawhney
Netaji Subhas Institute of Technology
Delhi, India
ramits.co@nsit.net.in

Debanjan Mahata
University of Arkansas at Little Rock
Arkansas, USA
dxmahata@ualr.edu

Abstract

The exponential rise of social media websites like Twitter, Facebook and Reddit in linguistically diverse geographical regions has led to hybridization of popular native languages with English in an effort to ease communication. The paper focuses on the classification of offensive tweets written in Hinglish language, which is a portmanteau of the Indic language Hindi with the Roman script. The paper introduces a novel tweet dataset, titled Hindi-English Offensive Tweet (HEOT) dataset, consisting of tweets in Hindi-English code switched language split into three classes: non-offensive, abusive and hate-speech. Further, we approach the problem of classification of the tweets in HEOT dataset using transfer learning wherein the proposed model employing Convolutional Neural Networks is pre-trained on tweets in English followed by retraining on Hinglish tweets.

1 Introduction

The rampant use of offensive content on social media is destructive to a progressive society as it tends to promote abuse, violence and chaos and severely impacts individuals at different levels. Offensive text can be broadly classified as abusive and hate speech on the basis of the context and target of the offense. Hate speech (Schmidt and Wiegand, 2017) is an act of offending, insulting or threatening a person or a group of similar people on the basis of religion, race, caste, sexual orientation, gender or belongingness to a specific stereotyped community. Abusive speech categorically differs from hate speech because of its casual motive to hurt using general slurs composed of demeaning words. Both abusive as well as hate speech are sub-categories of offensive speech.

Freedom of expression is one of the most aggressively contested rights of the modern world. While censorship of free moving online content such as Twitter tweets curtails the freedom of speech, but unregulated opprobrious tweets discourage free discussions in the virtual world (Silva et al., 2016). Hate speech detection is a hard research problem because of ambiguity in the clear demarcation of offensive, abusive and hateful textual content due to variations in the way people express themselves in a linguistically diverse social setting. A major challenge in monitoring online content produced on social media websites like Twitter, Facebook and Reddit is the humongous volume of data being generated at a fast pace from varying demographic, cultural, linguistic and religious communities.

A major contributor to the tremendously high offensive online content is *Hinglish* (Sreeram and Sinha, 2017), which is formed of the words spoken in Hindi language but written in Roman script instead of the Devanagari script. Hinglish is a pronunciation based bi-lingual language that has no fixed grammar rules.

Hinglish extends its grammatical setup from native Hindi accompanied by a plethora of slurs, slang and phonetic variations due to regional influence. Randomized spelling variations and mul-

Proceedings of the Sixth International Workshop on Natural Language Processing for Social Media , pages 18–26,
Melbourne, Australia, July 20, 2018. ©2018 Association for Computational Linguistics

tiple possible interpretations of Hinglish words in different contextual situations make it extremely difficult to deal with automatic classification of this language. Another challenge worth consideration in dealing with Hinglish is the demographic divide between the users of Hinglish relative to total active users globally. This poses a serious limitation as the tweet data in Hinglish language is a small fraction of the large pool of tweets generated, necessitating the use of selective methods to process such tweets in an automated fashion. We aim to solve the problem of detecting offensive Hinglish tweets through the development of a deep learning model that analyses the input text and segregates them as:

1. Not Offensive

2. Abusive

3. Hate-Inducing

A dataset of manually annotated Hinglish tweets is used to measure the performance of the proposed framework. The experimentation consists of two phases, the first of which investigates the semantic correlation of Hindi-English code switched language with native English language and proposes a dictionary-based translation of Hinglish text into Roman English text. Next, we analyze the performance of the semantically similar but syntactically different tweets obtained via transliteration and translation on a pre-trained Convolutional Neural Network (CNN) and propose improvements to the classical hate speech classification methodology through the transfer of previously learned features by the CNN. The main contributions of our work can be summarized as follows:

- Creation of an annotated dataset of Hinglish tweets

- Experimentation of transfer learning based neural networks for classifying tweets in Hinglish language as abusive, hate-inducing or non-Offensive.

2   Related Work

The voluminous data present on Twitter necessitates identification, ranking and segregation of event-specific informative content from the streams of trending tweets (Mahata et al., 2015). Orsini (2015) dates the origin of Hinglish as an informal language to postcolonial Indian society. Several work like that done by Dwivedi and Sukhadeve (2010) attempted to translate Hindi-English language into pure English. However, the major challenge in this case is that the grammatical rules of Hinglish are gravely uncertain and user dependent.

One of the earliest efforts in hate speech detection can be attributed to Spertus (1997) who had presented a decision tree based text classifier for web pages with a remarkable 88.2 % accuracy. Contemporary works on Yahoo news pages were done Sood et al. (2012) and later taken up by Yin et al. (2016a) . Xiang et al. (2012) detected offensive tweets using logistic regression over a tweet dataset with the help of a dictionary of 339 offensive words. Offensive text classification in other online textual content have been tried previously for other languages as well like German (Ross et al., 2017) and Arabic (Mubarak et al., 2017). However, despite the various endeavors by language experts and online moderators, users continue to disguise their abuse through creative modifications that contribute to multidimensional linguistic variations (Clarke and Grieve, 2017).

Badjatiya et al. (2017) used CNN based classifiers to classify hateful tweets as racist and sexist. Park and Fung (2017) introduced a combination of CharCNN and WordCNN architectures for abusive text classification. Gambäck and Sikdar (2017) explored four CNN models trained on character n-grams, word vectors based on semantic information built using word2vec, randomly generated word vectors, and word vectors combined with character n-grams to develop a hate-speech text classification system. Mahata et al. (2018) experimented with multi-channel CNN, BiLSTM and CNN+BiLSTM models for identifying specific posts from a large dataset of Twitter posts. Another interesting attempt in the same direction was made by Pitsilis et al. (2018) through an ensemble model of Recurrent Neural Network (RNN) classifiers.

3   Dataset

Table 1 shows the tweet distribution in English dataset A provided byDavidson et al. (2017) and the manually created Hinglish dataset HEOT. Dataset A consists of 14509 tweets such that 7274 are non-offensive, 4836 are abusive and 2399 are hate-inducing tweets. The imbalance of dataset is

Label	Dataset A	Dataset HEOT
Non-Offensive	7274	1414
Abusive	4836	1942
Hate-inducing	2399	323
Total	14509	3679

Table 1: Tweet distribution in dataset A and HEOT.

encouraged to represent a realistic picture usually seen on social media websites.

Dataset HEOT was created using the Twitter Streaming API by selecting tweets in Hindi-English code switched language by data mining specific profane words in Hinglish language. The tweets were collected during the months of November-December 2017 and were crowdsourced to ten NLP researchers for annotation and verification. The data repository thus created consists of 3679 tweets out of which the count of non-offensive, abusive and hate-inducing tweets is 1414, 1942 and 323 respectively and categorized similar to the previous dataset. Dataset HEOT is considerably small as compared to dataset A, but this abnormality is rather advantageous for our research. It is a common observation that online users who identify to a particular demographic subdivision are often a small percentage of the total active users. This restriction of the size of Hinglish corpus closely represents a true world scenario where the relative balance of standard and indigenous users is naturally skewed. Care was taken to ensure that the tweets having insufficient textual content were not incorporated into the dataset.

An illustration of the three types of tweets is presented below to explain the contextual meaning of each class label in different languages. The tweets in category 1, 2 and 3 are non-offensive, abusive and hate-inducing respectively. In the examples given here, each tweet belonging to class A and B is in English and Hinglish language respectively. The tweets that fall under class C exemplify the corresponding version of Hinglish tweets after transliteration, translation and preprocessing.

1. (a) We all are going outside? http://t...
   (b) Hum sab ghumne jaa rahe hain? http://t...
   (c) we all outside go are

2. (a) @username1 B*tch! Do not teach me:/
   (b) @username1 Kutiya! Mujhe mat sikha:/
   (c) b*tch me not teach

3. (a) M*th*rf*ck*r Kill terrorist Akbaar #SaveWorld
   (b) M*d*rch*d aatanki Akbaar ko maara daalo #SaveWorld
   (c) m*th*rf*ck*r terrorist Akbaar kill

Hinglish to Devanagari Hindi transliteration was done by using the datasets provided by Khapra et al. (2014), while the Hindi to Roman English translation was achieved by using the Hindi-English dictionary sourced from CFILT, IIT Bombay[1]. A crowdsourced list of 208 profane Hinglish words along with their spelling variations, regional dialects, homonyms and contextual variants were added to the corpus of 7193 word-pairs to be used for all the Hinglish to English tweet conversions discussed in this paper.

4 Methodology

4.1 Preprocessing

The tweets obtained from data sources were channeled through a pre-processing pipeline with the ultimate aim to transform them into semantic feature vectors.

The transliteration process was broken into intermediate steps:

1. Removal of punctuations, URLs and user mentions.

2. Replacement of hashtags with corresponding plain text.

3. Replacement of emoticons with appropriate textual descriptions sourced from the list provided by Agarwal et al. (2011).

4. Conversion of all tweets into lower case.

5. Removal of useless words providing little textual information using stop words obtained from Gensim (Rehurek and Sojka, 2011).

6. Translation of Hinglish words into corresponding English words.

---

[1] `http://www.cfilt.iitb.ac.in/~hdict/webinterface_user/`

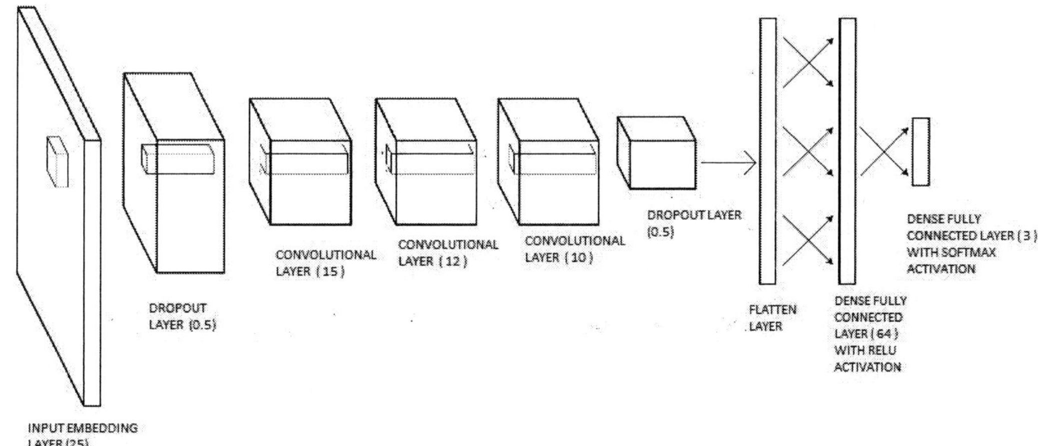

Figure 1: Convolutional Neural Network (CNN) architecture used for Ternary Trans-CNN model

7. Transformation of pre-processed tweets into a word vector representation through Glove (Pennington et al., 2014) pre-trained vector embeddings. The version of Glove pre trained word vectors used in our case was Twitter (2B tweets, 27B tokens, 1.2M vocab, uncased, 200d, 1.42 GB download).

8. The final step in tweet transformation was the creation a word vector sequences that can be fed into the neural network architecture.

4.2 Transfer Learning

Transfer learning (Pan and Yang, 2010) is a machine learning paradigm that refers to knowledge transfer from one domain of interest to another, with the aim to reuse already learned features in learning a specialized task. The task from which the system extracts knowledge is referred to as source task while the task which benefits is termed as target task. Such representation learning systems are used in cases where the feature space and distribution of input are similar so as to get maximum benefit from the knowledge transfer exercise. Another pertinent role of transfer learning is data reclassification without overfitting in cases where data extraction restraints the size of training data.

Bengio (2012) put emphasis on two predominant cases which are well suited for the application of transfer learning. The first case is when the class labels of source and target task vary but the input distribution is same. The other is when the class labels are similar but the input distribu-tion varies. The proposed problem of hate speech detection in Hinglish tweets is a classic example of the second case due to the semantic parallelism between English and translated Hinglish language, despite the eventual grammatical disassociation when Hinglish is transliterated into Roman script. Transfer learning provides relative performance increase at a reduced storage and computational cost.

Pan and Yang (2010) gave a mathematical definition of transfer learning and justified use cases for application of transfer learning. Let domain D consist of two components: a feature space X and a marginal probability distribution $P(X)$, where $X = \{x_1, x_2, \cdots, x_n\} \in X$, X is the space of all individual word vectors representing the input text, x_i is the ith vector corresponding to some tweet and X is a particular learning sample. A task consists of two components: a label space Y and an objective predictive function $f()$, represented as $T = \{Y, f()\}$, which is not observed but can be learned from the training data, which consists of pairs (x_i, y_i), where $x_i \in X$ and $y_i \in Y$. In the experiments, Y is the set of all labels for a multi-class classification task, and y_i is one of three class labels. Figure 1 shows the architecture of convolutional neural network used in the experiments throughout the paper. CNN models pre-trained on English dataset learn low-level features of the English language. The last few layers are removed and then replaced with fresh layers keeping the initial convolutional layers frozen and retrained on dataset HEOT where it learns to ex-

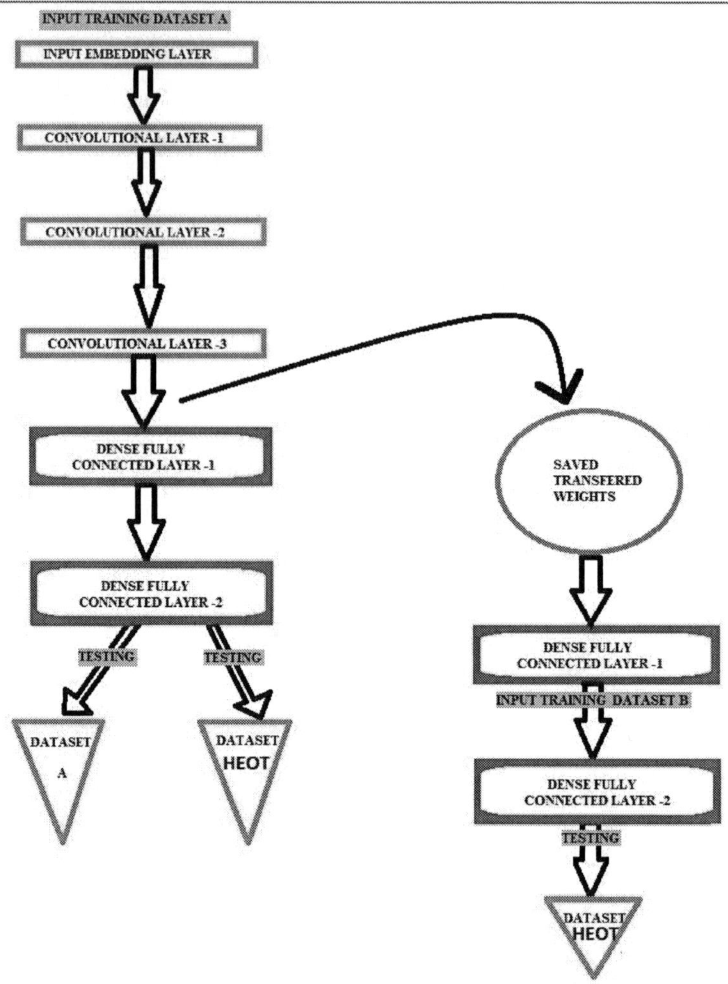

Figure 2: Transfer learning technique used for Ternary Trans-CNN model

tract intricate features due to syntax variations in pre-processed Hinglish text.

5 Proposed Approach

The authors have put forward an experimental schema for Hinglish hate speech classification, termed as Ternary Trans-CNN model.

5.1 Ternary Trans-CNN Model

Ternary Trans-CNN model aims to achieve the three-label classification of Hinglish tweets using transfer learning on a pre-trained CNN architecture depicted in Figure 2. The model is trained successively on English dataset A and Hinglish dataset HEOT. We have empirically chosen embedding dimension to be 200. The proposed CNN architecture consists of 3 layers of Convolutional1D layers having filter size 15,12 and 10 respectively and kernel size fixed to 3. The last two layers are dense fully-connected layers with size 64 and 3 units and the activation function as Rectified Linear Unit (ReLU) (Maas et al., 2013) and 'Softmax' respectively. The loss function used is categorical cross-entropy on account of multi-label classification role of the model. We used Adam optimizer (Kingma and Ba, 2014)

The batch size was experimented from size 8 to 256 using grid search. Similarly, the number of epochs were chosen by exploring different values from 10 to 50. The number of trainable and static layers varied to get the best combination giving optimal results. To ensure that the models do not overfit, dropout layers after the dense layers were

Dataset	A	HEOT (w/o TFL)	HEOT (TFL)
Accuracy (%)	75.40	58.70	83.90
Precision	0.672	0.556	0.802
Recall	0.644	0.473	0.698
F1 Score	0.643	0.427	0.714

Table 2: Results for Ternary Trans-CNN task: non-offensive, abusive and hate-inducing tweet classification on datasets A, HEOT without transfer learning (w/o TFL) and HEOT with transfer learning (TFL)

introduced to enhance generalization of the systems. The Ternary Trans-CNN model is initially trained on 11509 training data points and tested on 3000 data points that were randomly split from the parent dataset A. The batch size is set to 128 for 25 epochs with all layers as trainable. The same model is retrained, keeping only last two layers as trainable and other layers frozen, on dataset HEOT which is split into 2679 training and 1000 testing examples. The batch size was decreased to 64 with epochs reduced to 10 for minimum training loss and the metric measurements were recorded in Table 2 for further comparative analysis.

6 RESULTS AND ANALYSIS

The results of Ternary Trans-CNN model were compiled in terms of accuracy, F1 score, precision, and recall by choosing macro metrics as the class imbalance is not severe enough to strongly bias the outcomes. The CNN model was initially trained on dataset A and its performance on it taken as the baseline. Testing the same model on dataset HEOT without transfer learning reports downfall in model performance as compared to the baseline which is justified because the Hinglish tweets in dataset HEOT suffer from syntactic degradation after transliteration and translation which leads to a loss in the contextual structuring of the tweets. After retraining the Trans-CNN model, the model performance on dataset HEOT not only improves significantly but also surpasses the earlier results on dataset A. Thus, we can safely conclude that there was a positive transfer of features from source to target data.

7 CONCLUSION AND FUTURE WORK

This work demonstrates various CNN based models for multi-class labeling of offensive textual tweets. An important contribution of the paper is to analyze informal languages on social media such as Hinglish for hate speech and suggest ways to transform them into English text for the purpose of natural language processing. The dataset provided is an optimistic step in contribution to the study of code-switched languages such as Hinglish that play a major role in online social structuring of multi-linguistic societies. The experiments prove that a positive transfer of knowledge and characteristics between two congruent domains is made possible by training, freezing and retraining the models from source to target tasks. The success of transfer learning for analyzing complex cross linguistic textual structures can be extended to include many more tasks involving code-switched and code-mixed data.

The future efforts can be directed towards fine-tuning the neural network models using boosting methods such as gradient boosting (Badjatiya et al., 2017). The experiments here used CNN models for primary training, but other types of deep learning models like LSTM have also been known to show a high affinity for semantic tasks such as sentiment analysis (Wang et al., 2016) and sentence translation (Sutskever et al., 2014). Another possible approach to fine-tune the classification can be to use a stacked ensemble of shallow convolutional neural network (CNN) models as shown by Friedrichs et al. (2018).

In recent years, leveraging multimodal information in several multimedia analytics problem has shown great success (Shah, 2016a,b; Shah and Zimmermann, 2017). Thus, in the future, we plan to exploit multimodal information in offensive language detection since the most of existing systems work in unimodal settings. Moreover, since offensive language is closely related with sentiments, keywords (or hashtags), and some associated events, we would also like to explore aspects (Jangid et al., 2018), tag relevance (Shah et al., 2016a,b), and events (Shah et al., 2015a,

2016c) for the present problem. Furthermore, we would like extend our work to build an offensive video segmentation system (Shah et al., 2014a, 2015b) in order to filter abusive and hate-inciting videos on social media. Since offensive code-switched languages are heavily influenced by region (*i.e.*, location), we would try to exploit the location information of videos as well in our extended work (Shah et al., 2014b,c; Yin et al., 2016b). Finally, since relative positions of words play a pivotal role in analyzing Hindi, we would like explore such possibilities in our future work (Shaikh et al., 2013a,b).

References

Apoorv Agarwal, Boyi Xie, Ilia Vovsha, Owen Rambow, and Rebecca Passonneau. 2011. Sentiment analysis of twitter data. In *Proceedings of the workshop on languages in social media*, pages 30–38. Association for Computational Linguistics.

Pinkesh Badjatiya, Shashank Gupta, Manish Gupta, and Vasudeva Varma. 2017. Deep learning for hate speech detection in tweets. In *Proceedings of the 26th International Conference on World Wide Web Companion*, pages 759–760. International World Wide Web Conferences Steering Committee.

Yoshua Bengio. 2012. Deep learning of representations for unsupervised and transfer learning. In *Proceedings of ICML Workshop on Unsupervised and Transfer Learning*, pages 17–36.

Isobelle Clarke and Jack Grieve. 2017. Dimensions of abusive language on twitter. In *Proceedings of the First Workshop on Abusive Language Online*, pages 1–10.

Thomas Davidson, Dana Warmsley, Michael Macy, and Ingmar Weber. 2017. Automated hate speech detection and the problem of offensive language. *arXiv preprint arXiv:1703.04009*.

Sanjay K Dwivedi and Pramod P Sukhadeve. 2010. Machine translation system in indian perspectives. *Journal of computer science*, 6(10):1111.

Jasper Friedrichs, Debanjan Mahata, and Shubham Gupta. 2018. Infynlp at smm4h task 2: Stacked ensemble of shallow convolutional neural networks for identifying personal medication intake from twitter. *arXiv preprint arXiv:1803.07718*.

Björn Gambäck and Utpal Kumar Sikdar. 2017. Using convolutional neural networks to classify hate-speech. In *Proceedings of the First Workshop on Abusive Language Online*, pages 85–90.

Hitkul Jangid, Shivangi Singhal, Rajiv Ratn Shah, and Roger Zimmermann. 2018. Aspect-based financial sentiment analysis using deep learning. In *Companion of the The Web Conference 2018 on The Web Conference 2018*, pages 1961–1966. International World Wide Web Conferences Steering Committee.

Mitesh M Khapra, Ananthakrishnan Ramanathan, Anoop Kunchukuttan, Karthik Visweswariah, and Pushpak Bhattacharyya. 2014. When transliteration met crowdsourcing: An empirical study of transliteration via crowdsourcing using efficient, non-redundant and fair quality control. In *LREC*, pages 196–202.

Diederik P Kingma and Jimmy Ba. 2014. Adam: A method for stochastic optimization. *arXiv preprint arXiv:1412.6980*.

Andrew L Maas, Awni Y Hannun, and Andrew Y Ng. 2013. Rectifier nonlinearities improve neural network acoustic models. In *Proc. icml*, volume 30, page 3.

Debanjan Mahata, Jasper Friedrichs, Rajiv Ratn Shah, et al. 2018. # phramacovigilance-exploring deep learning techniques for identifying mentions of medication intake from twitter. *arXiv preprint arXiv:1805.06375*.

Debanjan Mahata, John R Talburt, and Vivek Kumar Singh. 2015. From chirps to whistles: discovering event-specific informative content from twitter. In *Proceedings of the ACM web science conference*, page 17. ACM.

Hamdy Mubarak, Kareem Darwish, and Walid Magdy. 2017. Abusive language detection on arabic social media. In *Proceedings of the First Workshop on Abusive Language Online*, pages 52–56.

Francesca Orsini. 2015. Dil maange more: Cultural contexts of hinglish in contemporary india. *African Studies*, 74(2):199–220.

Sinno Jialin Pan and Qiang Yang. 2010. A survey on transfer learning. *IEEE Transactions on knowledge and data engineering*, 22(10):1345–1359.

Ji Ho Park and Pascale Fung. 2017. One-step and two-step classification for abusive language detection on twitter. *arXiv preprint arXiv:1706.01206*.

Jeffrey Pennington, Richard Socher, and Christopher Manning. 2014. Glove: Global vectors for word representation. In *Proceedings of the 2014 conference on empirical methods in natural language processing (EMNLP)*, pages 1532–1543.

Georgios K Pitsilis, Heri Ramampiaro, and Helge Langseth. 2018. Detecting offensive language in tweets using deep learning. *arXiv preprint arXiv:1801.04433*.

R Rehurek and P Sojka. 2011. Gensim–python framework for vector space modelling. *NLP Centre, Faculty of Informatics, Masaryk University, Brno, Czech Republic*, 3(2).

Björn Ross, Michael Rist, Guillermo Carbonell, Benjamin Cabrera, Nils Kurowsky, and Michael Wojatzki. 2017. Measuring the reliability of hate speech annotations: The case of the european refugee crisis. *arXiv preprint arXiv:1701.08118*.

Anna Schmidt and Michael Wiegand. 2017. A survey on hate speech detection using natural language processing. In *Proceedings of the Fifth International Workshop on Natural Language Processing for Social Media*, pages 1–10.

Rajiv Ratn Shah. 2016a. Multimodal analysis of user-generated content in support of social media applications. In *Proceedings of the ACM International Conference on Multimedia Retrieval*, pages 423–426.

Rajiv Ratn Shah. 2016b. Multimodal-based multimedia analysis, retrieval, and services in support of social media applications. In *Proceedings of the ACM International Conference on Multimedia*, pages 1425–1429.

Rajiv Ratn Shah, Anupam Samanta, Deepak Gupta, Yi Yu, Suhua Tang, and Roger Zimmermann. 2016a. PROMPT: Personalized user tag recommendation for social media photos leveraging multimodal information. In *Proceedings of the ACM International Conference on Multimedia*, pages 486–492.

Rajiv Ratn Shah, Anwar Dilawar Shaikh, Yi Yu, Wenjing Geng, Roger Zimmermann, and Gangshan Wu. 2015a. EventBuilder: Real-time multimedia event summarization by visualizing social media. In *Proceedings of the ACM International Conference on Multimedia*, pages 185–188.

Rajiv Ratn Shah, Yi Yu, Anwar Dilawar Shaikh, Suhua Tang, and Roger Zimmermann. 2014a. ATLAS: Automatic temporal segmentation and annotation of lecture videos based on modelling transition time. In *Proceedings of the ACM International Conference on Multimedia*, pages 209–212.

Rajiv Ratn Shah, Yi Yu, Anwar Dilawar Shaikh, and Roger Zimmermann. 2015b. TRACE: A linguistic-based approach for automatic lecture video segmentation leveraging Wikipedia texts. In *Proceedings of the IEEE International Symposium on Multimedia*, pages 217–220.

Rajiv Ratn Shah, Yi Yu, Suhua Tang, Shin'ichi Satoh, Akshay Verma, and Roger Zimmermann. 2016b. Concept-level multimodal ranking of Flickr photo tags via recall based weighting. In *Proceedings of the MMCommon's Workshop at ACM International Conference on Multimedia*, pages 19–26.

Rajiv Ratn Shah, Yi Yu, Akshay Verma, Suhua Tang, Anwar Shaikh, and Roger Zimmermann. 2016c. Leveraging multimodal information for event summarization and concept-level sentiment analysis. *Knowledge-Based Systems*, 108:102–109.

Rajiv Ratn Shah, Yi Yu, and Roger Zimmermann. 2014b. ADVISOR: Personalized video soundtrack recommendation by late fusion with heuristic rankings. In *Proceedings of the ACM International Conference on Multimedia*, pages 607–616.

Rajiv Ratn Shah, Yi Yu, and Roger Zimmermann. 2014c. User preference-aware music video generation based on modeling scene moods. In *Proceedings of the ACM International Conference on Multimedia Systems*, pages 156–159.

Rajiv Ratn Shah and Roger Zimmermann. 2017. *Multimodal Analysis of User-Generated Multimedia Content*. Springer.

Anwar D Shaikh, Mukul Jain, Mukul Rawat, Rajiv Ratn Shah, and Manoj Kumar. 2013a. Improving accuracy of SMS based FAQ retrieval system. In *Proceedings of the Springer Multilingual Information Access in South Asian Languages*, pages 142–156.

Anwar Dilawar Shaikh, Rajiv Ratn Shah, and Rahis Shaikh. 2013b. SMS based FAQ retrieval for Hindi, English and Malayalam. In *Proceedings of the ACM Forum on Information Retrieval Evaluation*, page 9.

Leandro Araújo Silva, Mainack Mondal, Denzil Correa, Fabrício Benevenuto, and Ingmar Weber. 2016. Analyzing the targets of hate in online social media. In *ICWSM*, pages 687–690.

Sara Owsley Sood, Elizabeth F Churchill, and Judd Antin. 2012. Automatic identification of personal insults on social news sites. *Journal of the Association for Information Science and Technology*, 63(2):270–285.

Ellen Spertus. 1997. Smokey: Automatic recognition of hostile messages. In *AAAI/IAAI*, pages 1058–1065.

Ganji Sreeram and Rohit Sinha. 2017. Language modeling for code-switched data: Challenges and approaches. *arXiv preprint arXiv:1711.03541*.

Ilya Sutskever, Oriol Vinyals, and Quoc V Le. 2014. Sequence to sequence learning with neural networks. In *Advances in neural information processing systems*, pages 3104–3112.

Jin Wang, Liang-Chih Yu, K Robert Lai, and Xuejie Zhang. 2016. Dimensional sentiment analysis using a regional cnn-lstm model. In *Proceedings of the 54th Annual Meeting of the Association for Computational Linguistics (Volume 2: Short Papers)*, volume 2, pages 225–230.

Guang Xiang, Bin Fan, Ling Wang, Jason Hong, and Carolyn Rose. 2012. Detecting offensive tweets via topical feature discovery over a large scale twitter corpus. In *Proceedings of the 21st ACM international conference on Information and knowledge management*, pages 1980–1984. ACM.

Dawei Yin, Yuening Hu, Jiliang Tang, Tim Daly, Mianwei Zhou, Hua Ouyang, Jianhui Chen, Changsung Kang, Hongbo Deng, Chikashi Nobata, et al. 2016a. Ranking relevance in yahoo search. In *Proceedings of the 22nd ACM SIGKDD International Conference on Knowledge Discovery and Data Mining*, pages 323–332. ACM.

Yifang Yin, Rajiv Ratn Shah, and Roger Zimmermann. 2016b. A general feature-based map matching framework with trajectory simplification. In *Proceedings of the 7th ACM SIGSPATIAL International Workshop on GeoStreaming*, page 7.

SocialNLP 2018 EmotionX Challenge Overview:
Recognizing Emotions in Dialogues

Chao-Chun Hsu[1]   **Lun-Wei Ku**[1,2]

[1] Academia Sinica, Taiwan.

`{joe32140,lwku}@iis.sinica.edu.tw`

[2] Joint Research Center for AI Technology and All Vista Healthcare, Taiwan.

Abstract

This paper describes an overview of the Dialogue Emotion Recognition Challenge, EmotionX, at the Sixth SocialNLP Workshop, which recognizes the emotion of each utterance in dialogues. This challenge offers the EmotionLines dataset as the experimental materials. The Emotion-Lines dataset contains conversations from Friends TV show transcripts (Friends) and real chatting logs (EmotionPush), where every dialogue utterance is labeled with emotions. Organizers provide baseline results. 18 teams registered in this challenge and 5 of them submitted their results successfully. The best team achieves the unweighted accuracy 62.48 and 62.5 on EmotionPush and Friends, respectively. In this paper we present the task definition, test collection, the evaluation results of the groups that participated in this challenge, and their approaches.

1 Introduction

Human emotion underlays in our daily interactions with other people, and study from Ekman(1987) shows that emotion is a universal phenomena across different cultures. An emotion detection system can improve mutual understanding between individuals by providing undetected emotion signal. For a common sense of human perception that emotion is inherently multi-modality including vision and speech, multi-modal emotion recognition plays an important role in emotion detection area(Sebe et al.; Kessous et al., 2010; Haq and Jackson, 2011). At the same time, studies in uni-modal emotion recognition also contribute in variety of modalities like vision(Ekman and Friesen, 2003), speech(Nwe et al., 2003) and text(Alm et al., 2005).

Chandler	Matthew Perry talking about signs in Las Vegas. (Neutral)
Chandler	I guess it must've been some movie I saw. (Neutral)
Chandler	What do you say? (Neutral)
Monica	*Okay! (Joy)*
Chandler	Okay! Come on! Let's go! All right! (Joy)
Rachel	Oh okay, I'll fix that to. What's her e-mail address? (Neutral)
Ross	Rachel! (Anger)
Rachel	All right, I promise. I'll fix this. I swear. I'll-I'll- I'll-I'll talk to her. (Non-neutral)
Ross	*Okay! (Anger)*
Rachel	Okay. (Neutral)

Table 1: "Okay!" of different emotions from Emotionlines dataset.

However, with the progress of social media and dialogue systems, especially the online customer services, textual emotion recognition has attracted more attention. In the social media, the hashtag and emoji are widely used and could provide substantial emotion clues(Qadir and Riloff, 2014; Kralj Novak et al., 2015). For the dialogue systems, instant emotion detection could help costumer service notice dissatisfaction of clients. Still, textual emotion recognition needs further exploration in dialogue systems for many reasons. For instance, a text segment can express various emotions given different context. Take the dialogue from Hsu et al.(2018) in Table 1 as an example, *Okay!* could be joy or anger in different scenarios. One more reason is that informal language and short sentence are everywhere in daily conversation. For instance, *lol* actually means *laugh out loud*. Therefore, emotion flow modeling and informal language understanding are essential for improving dialogue emotion recognition system.

For EmotionX shared task in SocialNLP 2018, we select an emotional dialogue dataset, Emo-

Proceedings of the Sixth International Workshop on Natural Language Processing for Social Media , pages 27–31,
Melbourne, Australia, July 20, 2018. ©2018 Association for Computational Linguistics

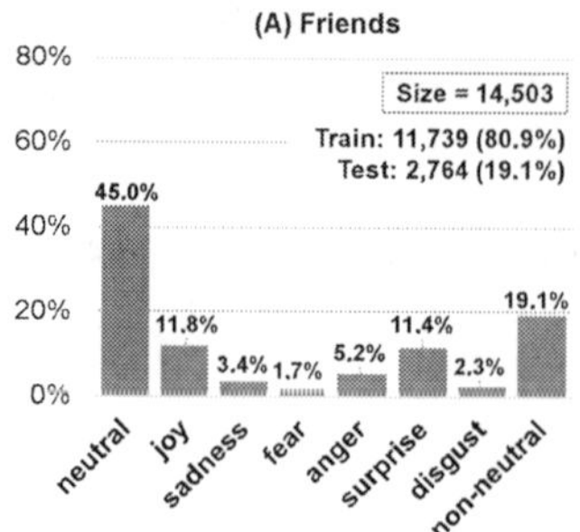

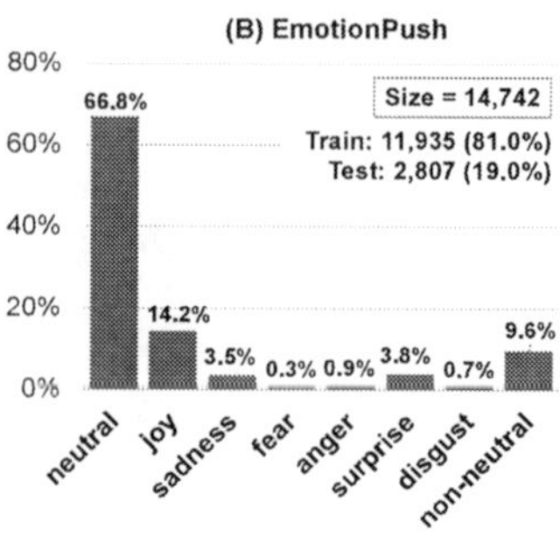

Figure 1: Emotion label distribution of Friends and EmotionPush datasets

tionlines, as the challenge dataset. A total of five teams presented their approaches, including feature-based and learning-based models, in this task. Neural models such as convolutional neural network(CNN) and recurrent neural network appear in all teams' work. The winning system achieves the unweighted accuracy 62.5% and 62.48% on Friends and EmotionPush dataset in the Emotionlines.

2 EmotionLines Dataset

EmotionLines is collected from two sources: Friends TV show transcripts (Friends) and Facebook messenger logs (EmotionPush). Dialogues are randomly selected from the raw data in four buckets of dialogue length [4-9], [10-14], [15-29], and [20-24], with 250 dialogues for each bucket. However, EmotionPush is a private chat log and releasing it may encounter privacy issues. To cope with this problem, Stanford Named Entity Recognizer (Manning et al., 2014) was adopted to replace the named entities in the corpus. In (Hsu et al., 2018), Amazon Mechanical Turk is utilized to label the emotion of every utterance. Following Ekman's(1987) six basic emotions and with neutral added, seven emotions are available for annotators in the labeling interface. To eliminate diverse emotion-labeled utterances, the utterance annotated with more than two emotions is considered as the non-neutral utterance. Finally, a total of eight emotion labels in both Friends and EmotionPush datasets are joy, anger, sadness, surprise, fear, disgust, neutral, and non-neutral. Figure 1 shows the emotion label distribution for these two datasets.

As we can see, more than 45% utterances are of neural emotion labels in both datasets, and the more severe emotion label imbalance in EmotionPush reflects the real situation that most of the utterances are neutral in daily conversations.

3 Challenge Setup

In shared task, each dataset is split into the training, the validation, and the testing set with 720, 80, 200 dialogues respectively. Due to the very few utterances of some emotions, we only evaluate the performance of recognizing four emotions: Joy, Anger, Sadness, Neutral, which was announced in the early announcement during the challenge. Generally speaking, recognizing strong emotions may provide more value than detecting the neutral emotion. To making a meaningful comparison in this challenge, we chose the unweighted accuracy(UWA) as our metric instead of the weighted accuracy(WA) as the latter is heavily compromised by the large proportion of the neutral emotion.

$$\text{WA} = \sum_{l \in C} s_l a_l \tag{1}$$

$$\text{UWA} = \frac{1}{|C|} \sum_{l \in C} a_l \tag{2}$$

where a_l denotes the accuracy of emotion class l and s_l denotes the percentage of utterances in emotion class l.

4 Submission

We receive 18 registrations and 5 teams submit their results successfully in the end. In the following, we summarize the approaches proposed by these 5 teams. More details could be found in their challenge papers.

Rank	Team	Model	Pre-trained Embedding	Other Resource	UWA (Friends)	UWA (EmotionPush)
1	**AR**	CNN	GloVe	Warriner's, NRC, PERMA lexicons, formal list	62.5	62.48
2	**DLC**	LSTM+Attension	GloVe	-	59.65	55
2	**Area66**	Hierarchical LSTM +Attention+CRF	GloVe	-	55.38	56.73
4	**SmartDubai**	Logistic regression	fastText*	-	25.53	26.55
-	**JTML**	CNN+Attension	GloVe	-	33.35	46.75

Table 2: Overview of methods proposed by the participants and UWA of both datasets. JTML team is not in the ranking list because of late submission. * SmartDubai only used word and character TF-IDF as features for logistics regression. fastText is used by their other framework.

	Friends				EmotionPush			
	Neutral	Anger	Joy	Sadness	Neutral	Anger	Joy	Sadness
AR	68.3	**55.3**	**71.1**	**55.3**	76.3	**45.9**	**76**	51.7
DLC	90.1	49.1	68.8	30.6	94.2	24.3	70.5	31
Area66	73.5	39.8	57.6	50.6	88.2	21.6	63.1	**54**
SmartDubai	**99.5**	0	2.6	0	**99**	0	7.2	0
JTML	85.2	3.1	45.1	0	91.4	0	65.7	29.9

Table 3: Accuracy of four emotions on Friends and EmotionPush datasets.

DLC (Hang Seng Management College) A self-attentive BiLSTM network inspired by Transformer(Vaswani et al., 2017) is proposed. The self-attentive architecture on the top of BiLSTM could provide information between utterances and BiLSTM tries to model the word dependency in each utterance. Emoji symbols are converted to their meaning.

AR (Adobe Research) A CNN-DCNN autoencoder based emotion classifier is proposed. The latent feature of CNN-DCNN is augmented with linguistic features, such as lexical , syntactic, derived, and psycho-linguistic features as well as the formality list. The joint training of the classifer and the autoencoder improves generalizability, and linguistic features boost the performance on the minority class. AR is the only team that considers imbalance of emotions and also the only team that does not use the context information.

SmartDubai NLP (Smart Dubai Government Establishment) Multiple approaches are implemented by this team including logistic regression, Naive Bayes, CNN-LSTM, Xgboost, where they select TF-IDF, word vector, and some NLP features to train their models. In addition, the Internet slang is converted to its meaning e.g. *lol* is replaced by *lots of laughs*. Finally, logistic regression with TF-IDF of words and characters reached highest performance.

Area66 (TCS Research) A hierarchical attention network with a conditional random fields (CRF) layer on top of it is proposed. The word embeddings of the utterance are fed in to LSTM, then the attention mechanism captures the words with important emotion representations to form the sentence embedding. To model the context dependency, utterance embeddings of the dialogue are passed through another LSTM and CRF layer to predict emotion of utterances.

JTML (ESPOL University) A classifier using 1-dimensional CNN to extract utterance features with attention mechanism across utterances which obtains context information is provided. The proposed GRU-Attention model uses sequential GRU to learn relationship between previous utterances and current utterance. It achieves an improvement on UWA.

5 Evaluation Results

A brief summary of approaches proposed by teams participated in the EmotionX challenge and their corresponding final results are shown in Table 2. The performance varies across teams. Especially, in Table 3, we observed that SmartDubai and JTML obtained lower UWA scores because of the low accuracy on the minority emotion classes such as anger and sadness. In contrast, the winning team AR successfully reached a similar performance on four emotions on both datasets.

6 Discussion

6.1 Word Embedding

All teams used pre-trained word embedding: GloVe(Pennington et al., 2014) for four teams and fastText(Joulin et al., 2016) for one team. Area66 used GloVe-Tweet which is more related to informal language and the other teams did not mention the pre-trained data in their papers. Using pre-trained word embedding can reduce the unseen word issue in the testing phase especially for the relatively small dataset (Friends and EmotionPush only contain $\sim$ 14,000 utterances, which is small compared to the commonly used datasets for pre-training the embedding.)

6.2 Neural Network

Neural network architectures are adopted in all challenge papers. Acting as a universal feature extractor, neural network could minimize the feature engineering process. AR and JTML apply CNN to generate utterance embedding , and Area66 and DLC choose LSTM instead. By modeling context information in dialogue, DLC shows that self-attention improves UWA performance on both datasets. In addition, the AR team finds that adding a reconstruction loss of DCNN could improve generalizability.

6.3 Linguistic Features

Team AR combines latent feature of CNN-DCNN and linguistic features to prediction utterance emotion. Also, AR is the only team leveraging external resources, e.g. lexicons and the formal list. By adding linguistic features into neural model, the accuracy of anger is significantly boosted by 8.2% and 33.3% on Friends and EmotionPush, respectively. For the SmartDubai team, they use word and character TF-IDF independently with logistic regression. Results show it suppresses the Xgboost using TF-IDF and some linguistic features, e.g. sentence length and percentage of unique words, and outperforms CNN-BiLSTM using fastText word embedding, too.

6.4 Data Imbalance

Data imbalance directly harm the UWA performance. In Table 3, accuracy of minority emotions like anger and sadness are relatively low for SmartDubai and JTML, leading to low UWA performance. In contrast, AR is the only team considering data imbalance in the training process. They achieve balance accuracy on each emotion by applying weighed loss in the loss function , and ultimately obtain the best performance in the EmotionX challenge.

7 Conclusion

We have a succesfull dialogue emotion recognition challenge, EmotionX, in SocialNLP 2018. Many researchers have noticed this challenge and requested the datasets. Moreover, 5 teams successfully submitted their results this year. Various interesting approaches are proposed for this challenge, and the best performance achieves the unweighted accuracy 62.5% and 62.48% on Friends and EmotionPush dataset in the Emotionlines. We will continue organizing this challenge in SocialNLP 2019 and have planned to add the subtask of emotion dialogue generation, in the hope of encouraging and facilitating the research community to work on the emotion analysis on dialogues.

8 Acknowledgement

This research is partially supported by Ministry of Science and Technology, Taiwan, under Grant no. MOST 106-2218-E-002-043-, 107-2634-F-002-011- and 107-2634-F-001-004-. We especially thank Ting-Hao (Kenneth) Huang for deploying Amazon Mechanical Turk experiments and providing the figure of the emotion label distribution.

References

Cecilia Ovesdotter Alm, Dan Roth, and Richard Sproat. 2005. Emotions from text: machine learning for text-based emotion prediction. In *Proceedings of the conference on human language technology and empirical methods in natural language processing*, pages 579–586. Association for Computational Linguistics.

Paul Ekman and Wallace V Friesen. 2003. *Unmasking the face: A guide to recognizing emotions from facial clues*. Ishk.

Paul Ekman, Wallace V Friesen, Maureen O'sullivan, Anthony Chan, Irene Diacoyanni-Tarlatzis, Karl Heider, Rainer Krause, William Ayhan LeCompte, Tom Pitcairn, Pio E Ricci-Bitti, et al. 1987. Universals and cultural differences in the judgments of facial expressions of emotion. *Journal of personality and social psychology*, 53(4):712.

Sanaul Haq and Philip JB Jackson. 2011. Multimodal emotion recognition. In *Machine audition: principles, algorithms and systems*, pages 398–423. IGI Global.

Chao-Chun Hsu, Sheng-Yeh Chen, Chuan-Chun Kuo, Ting-Hao Huang, and Lun-Wei Ku. 2018. Emotionlines: An emotion corpus of multi-party conversations. In *Proceedings of the Eleventh International Conference on Language Resources and Evaluation, LREC 2018, Miyazaki, Japan, May 7-12, 2018*.

Armand Joulin, Edouard Grave, Piotr Bojanowski, Matthijs Douze, Hérve Jégou, and Tomas Mikolov. 2016. Fasttext.zip: Compressing text classification models. *arXiv preprint arXiv:1612.03651*.

Loic Kessous, Ginevra Castellano, and George Caridakis. 2010. Multimodal emotion recognition in speech-based interaction using facial expression, body gesture and acoustic analysis. *Journal on Multimodal User Interfaces*, 3(1-2):33–48.

Petra Kralj Novak, Jasmina Smailovi, Borut Sluban, and Igor Mozeti. 2015. Sentiment of emojis. *PLOS ONE*, 10(12):1–22.

Christopher D. Manning, Mihai Surdeanu, John Bauer, Jenny Finkel, Steven J. Bethard, and David McClosky. 2014. The Stanford CoreNLP natural language processing toolkit. In *Association for Computational Linguistics (ACL) System Demonstrations*, pages 55–60.

Tin Lay Nwe, Say Wei Foo, and Liyanage C De Silva. 2003. Speech emotion recognition using hidden markov models. *Speech communication*, 41(4):603–623.

Jeffrey Pennington, Richard Socher, and Christopher D. Manning. 2014. Glove: Global vectors for word representation. In *In EMNLP*.

Ashequl Qadir and Ellen Riloff. 2014. Learning emotion indicators from tweets: Hashtags, hashtag patterns, and phrases. In *Proceedings of the 2014 Conference on Empirical Methods in Natural Language Processing (EMNLP)*, pages 1203–1209.

Nicu Sebe, Ira Cohen, and Thomas S. Huang. *MULTIMODAL EMOTION RECOGNITION*.

Ashish Vaswani, Noam Shazeer, Niki Parmar, Jakob Uszkoreit, Llion Jones, Aidan N Gomez, Ł ukasz Kaiser, and Illia Polosukhin. 2017. Attention is all you need. In I. Guyon, U. V. Luxburg, S. Bengio, H. Wallach, R. Fergus, S. Vishwanathan, and R. Garnett, editors, *Advances in Neural Information Processing Systems 30*, pages 5998–6008. Curran Associates, Inc.

A Appendix

A.1 Registration Teams

EmotionX challenge obtained the attention of researchers including Amit Agarwal, Denis Lukovnikov, Egor Lakomkin, Fatiha Sadat, Gangeshwar Krishnamurthy, Gregory Grefenstette, Kushagra Singh, Pinelopi Papalampidi, Sashank Santhanam, Srishti Aggarwal, and Xiaolei Huang, who registered the challenge and obtained the dataset but failed to submit their results regretfully.

EmotionX-DLC: Self-Attentive BiLSTM for Detecting Sequential Emotions in Dialogues

Linkai Luo
Hang Seng
Management College
llk1896@gmail.com

Haiqin Yang
Hang Seng
Management College
hqyang@ieee.org

Francis Y. L. Chin
Hang Seng
Management College
francischin@hsmc.edu.hk

Abstract

In this paper, we propose a self-attentive bidirectional long short-term memory (SA-BiLSTM) network to predict multiple emotions for the EmotionX challenge. The BiLSTM exhibits the power of modeling the word dependencies, and extracting the most relevant features for emotion classification. Building on top of BiLSTM, the self-attentive network can model the contextual dependencies between utterances which are helpful for classifying the ambiguous emotions. We achieve 59.6 and 55.0 unweighted accuracy scores in the *Friends* and the *EmotionPush* test sets, respectively.

1 Introduction

Emotion detection plays a crucial role in developing a smart dialogue system such as a chit-chat conversational bot (Chen et al., 2018). As a typical sub-problem of sentence classification, emotion classification requires not only to understand sentence of a single utterance, but also capture the contextual information from the whole conversations.

The problems of sentence-level classification have been investigated heavily by means of deep neural networks, such as convolutional neural networks (CNN) (Kim, 2014), long short-term memory (LSTM) (Liu et al., 2016), and attention-based CNN (Kim et al., 2018). Additional soft attention layers (Bahdanau et al., 2014) are usually built on top of those networks, such that more attention will be paid to the most relevant words that lead to a better understanding of the sentence. LSTMs (Hochreiter and Schmidhuber, 1997) are also useful to model contextual dependencies. For example, a contextual LSTM model is proposed

to select the next sentence based on the former context (Ghosh et al., 2016), and a bidirectional LSTM (BiLSTM) is adopted to detect multiple emotions (Chen et al., 2018).

In this work, we utilize the self-attentive BiLSTM (SA-BiLSTM) model to predict multiple types of emotions for the given utterances in the dialogues. Our model imitates human's two-step procedures for classifying an utterance within the context, i.e., sentence understanding and contextual utterances dependence extraction. More specifically, we propose the bidirectional long short-term memory (BiLSTM) with the max-pooling architecture to embed the sentence into a fixed-size vector, as the BiLSTM network is capable of modeling the word dependencies in the sentence while the max-pooling helps to reduce the model size and obtains the most related features for emotion classification. Since data in this challenge is limited and specific words play significant role to classifying the corresponding emotion, we apply the self-attention network (Vaswani et al., 2017) to extract the dependence of all the utterances in the dialogue. Technically, the self-attention model computes the influence of utterance pairs and outputs the sentence embedding of one utterance by a weighted sum over all the utterances in the dialogue. The fully connected layers are then applied on the output sentence embedding to classify the corresponding emotion.

2 Model

Figure 1 presents our designed model architecture. First, the pre-trained 300-dimensional GloVe vectors (Pennington et al., 2014) are adopted to represent each word (token). A sentence (utterance) with m tokens is then represented by

$$S = (w_1, w_2 \ldots, w_m), \qquad (1)$$

Proceedings of the Sixth International Workshop on Natural Language Processing for Social Media , pages 32–36,
Melbourne, Australia, July 20, 2018. ©2018 Association for Computational Linguistics

where w_i is d-dimensional word embedding for the i-th tokens in the sentence.

Suppose a dialogue consists of n sentences, the input forms an $n \times m \times d$ tensor, M, see Figure 1. Via the process of sentence embedding (elaborated in Section 2.1), the tensor is converted to a $n \times 2l$ matrix U, where l is the number of the hidden units for each unidirectional LSTM. By applying the self-attentive network, we re-weight the sentence embedding matrix to U' with the same shape as U. Finally, fully connected layers are trained to establish the mapping between input U' and the output emotion labels.

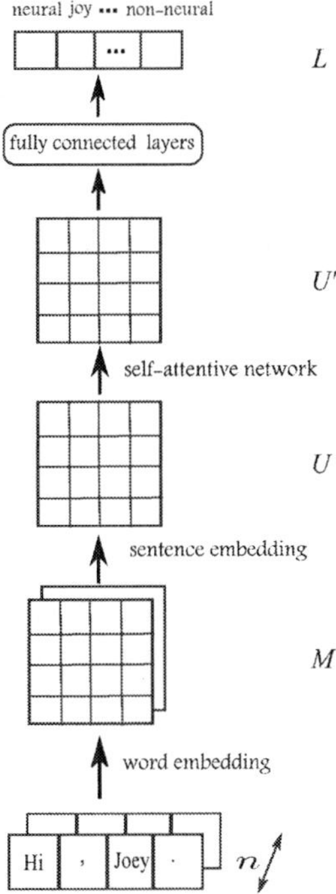

Figure 1: The model architecture illustration. A bunch of n utterances in one dialogue are processed through word embedding, sentence embedding, self-attentive and fully connected layers.

2.1 Sentence Embedding

In this work, we adopt the BiLSTM to learn the sentence embedding because it is the most popular neural network architecture to encode sentences (Conneau et al., 2017; Lin et al., 2017). The forward LSTM and backward LSTM read the sen-

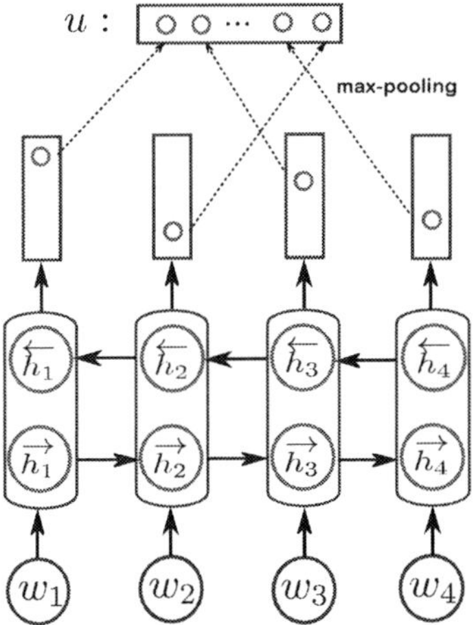

Figure 2: BiLSTM with max-pooling network.

tence S in two opposite directions (see Figure 2):

$$\overrightarrow{h}_t = \overrightarrow{LSTM}\left(w_t, \overrightarrow{h}_{t-1}\right) \tag{2}$$

$$\overleftarrow{h}_t = \overleftarrow{LSTM}\left(w_t, \overleftarrow{h}_{t+1}\right) \tag{3}$$

The vectors $\overrightarrow{h}_t$ and $\overleftarrow{h}_t$ are concatenated to a hidden state h_t. Max-pooling (Collobert and Weston, 2008) is then conducted along all the words of a sentence to output the final sentence representation, u.

2.2 The Self-attentive Network

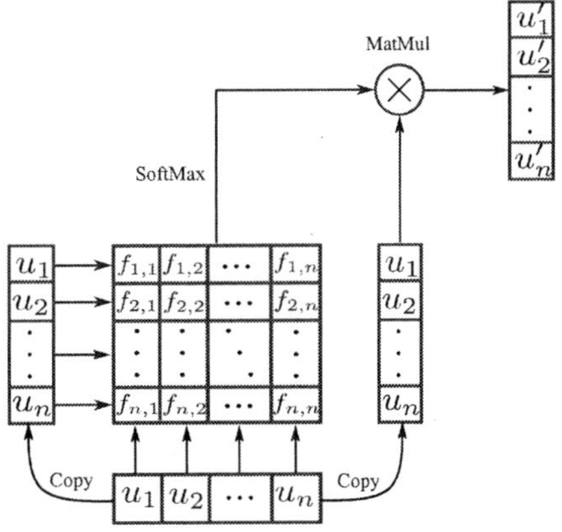

Figure 3: The self-attentive network. f_{ij} denotes $f(u_i, u_j)$ in Eq. 4.

The self-attention model, called Transformer (Vaswani et al., 2017), is an effective non-recurrent architecture for machine translation. We adopt it to capture the utterances dependence. Figure 3 shows the model to build the dot-product attention of utterances, where the attention matrix is calculated by:

$$f(u_i, u_j) = \begin{cases} \frac{u_i u_j^T}{\sqrt{d_k}}, & \text{if } i, j \leq n; \\ -\infty & \text{otherwise.} \end{cases} \quad (4)$$

where u_i is the i-th sentence embedding in the dialogue, and d_k (i.e. $2l$) is the model dimension. An attention mask is applied to waive the inner attention between sentence embeddings and paddings.

The i-th sentence embedding is finally weighted by summing over all the sentence embeddings to enhance the effect:

$$u_i' = \sum_j \text{softmax}\,(F_i)\, u_j, \quad (5)$$

where F_i is n-dimensional vector whose j-th element is $f(u_i, u_j)$.

2.3 Output and Loss

Finally, we apply fully connected layers to produce the corresponding emotions. In the training, the weighted cross-entropy is adopted as the loss function. Since the challenge only focuses on classifying four types of emotions, rather than all eight types, we set the weights to zero for the unconsidered emotions.

3 Experiments and Results

3.1 Data Preprocessing

The EmotionX dataset consists of the *Friends* TV scripts and the *EmotionPush* chat logs on Faceook Messenger in eight types, i.e., Neutral, Joy, Sadness, Anger, Fear, Surprise, Disgust and Nonneutral. For the train set, there are 720 dialogues for *Friends* and *EmotionPush*, respectively, which yields a total of 1,440 dialogues, 21,294 sentences, and 9,885 unique words. In the challenge, we test the following candidate labels, Neutral, Joy, Sadness, and Anger. We also conduct the following steps to clean the data:

- Unicode symbols, except emojis (the direct expressions of human emotions), are removed. Person names, locations, numbers and websites are replaced with special tokens.

- The Emoji symbols are converted to the corresponding meanings.

- Duplicated punctuation and symbols. Tokens with duplicated punctuation or alphabets, such as "oooooh", often imply non-neural emotions. We reconstruct the tokens to be `oh <duplicate>` to avoid informal words. The same rule also applies to similar tokens. For example, "oh!!!!!!" is replaced by `oh ! <duplicate>`.

- Word tokenization. We use NLTK's Twitter-Tokenizer (Bird, 2006) to split the sentences into tokens. All tokens are set lowercase.

3.2 Experimental Setup

We conduct two experiments with different model variants: BiLSTM and SA-BiLSTM, to validate whether our proposed model can learn the contextual information. The network settings for each model are summarized as follows:

- BiLSTM: BiLSTM + max-pooling + fully connected layers.

- SA-BiLSTM: BiLSTM + max-pooling + self-attentive network + fully connected layers.

The word embedding is 300-dimensional from the the Glove. Pack padded sequence and pad packed sequence are implemented to deal with varying sequence lengths. For SA-BiLSTM, we limit the utterance number to 25 for each dialogue. Due to the limit of training data, LSTM is set to one layer with only 256 hidden units. The fully connected layers consist of two middle layers with the same size of 128.

The mini-batch size for training BiLSTM is set to 16. Unlike BiLSTM, we feed one dialogue to SA-BiLSTM for every training step. Adam (Kingma and Ba, 2014) is the adopted optimizer with initial learning rate 0.0002 and decay factor 0.99 for every epoch. Dropout probability is set to 0.3 for BiLSTM and self-attention layers. We train BiLSTM for 10 epochs and SA-BiLSTM for 20 epochs to gain the best accuracy in the validation sets.

3.3 BiLSTM Versus SA-BiLSTM

Table 1 reports the model performance in the validation sets, which consist of 80 dialogues for *Friends* and *EmotionPush*, respectively. We evaluate two criteria, the weighted accuracy (WA) and the unweighted accuracy (UWA) (Chen et al.,

Model	Dataset	WA	UWA	Neutral	Joy	Sadness	Anger
BiLSTM	*Friends*	**79.4**	60.4	92.5	78.9	29.0	41.2
	EmotionPush	**83.9**	61.8	92.6	73.1	41.0	40.4
SA-BiLSTM	*Friends*	78.8	**62.8**	90.6	73.2	40.3	47.1
	EmotionPush	83.4	**63.5**	91.9	69.6	47.0	45.7

Table 1: Experimental results of *Friends* and *EmotionPush* in the validation sets.

Model	Dataset	UWA	Neutral	Joy	Sadness	Anger
SA-BiLSTM	*Friends*	59.6	90.1	68.8	30.6	49.1
	EmotionPush	55.0	94.2	70.5	31.0	24.3
	Average	57.3	92.1	69.6	30.8	36.7

Table 2: Experimental results of *Friends* and *EmotionPush* in the test sets.

2018). The predicted accuracy for each class is also given in the table.

Interestingly, the simpler model BiLSTM achieves higher WA, with up to 0.6% and 0.5% improvement in *Friends* and *EmotionPush*, respectively. On the other hand, SA-BiLSTM overperforms BiLSTM in terms of UWA, with up to 1.4% and 1.7% improvement. Note that BiLSTM tends to predict the emotions Neutral and Joy far more accurate than the other two emotions because most utterances are labeled as these two emotions, i.e., 45.03% as neural and 11.79% as joy in *Friends* while 66.85% as neural and 14.25% as joy in *EmotionPush*. Overall, SA-BiLSTM provides a more balanced prediction for each type of emotion than BiLSTM. Especially in predicting the emotions of Sadness and Anger, SA-BiLSTM gains better predictive accuracy, up to 11.3% & 6.0% on the Sadness emotion and 5.9% & 5.3% on the Anger emotion improvements in *Friends* and *EmotionPush*, respectively.

3.4 Results of Test Set

We submit the results produced by SA-BiLSTM and obtain the evaluation scores provided by the challenge organizer. Table 2 lists the experimental results evaluated in the test set, which consists of 400 dialogues, 200 dialogues for *Friends* and *EmotionPush*, respectively.

The results indicate that our model shows a strong bias towards predicting the Neutral emotion and the Joy emotion in both datasets compared to the Sadness and the Anger emotions. Especially, our model achieves an extremely poor prediction on the Anger emotion in *EmotionPush*. Moreover, the UWA in *EmotionPush* is smaller than that in *Friends*, which is different from our prediction results in the validation set. We conjecture that the distribution of the validation set and the test set may be slightly different. To obtain a robust solution, we may train multiple models using different random seeds and ensemble the model averaged on the checkpoints.

We notice that the *Speaker* information is also important for emotion classification. Table 3 shows two consecutive utterances made by the same speaker from *EmotionPush*, where the first utterance seems literally less emotional than the second one. Nevertheless, the two utterances should carry the same emotion, i.e., Anger, because they are made by the same speaker consecutively. On the contrary, our model gives a false prediction (i.e., Neutral) for the second utterance because it probably treats the two utterance separately. We believe that our model shall gain some improvements by adding speaker information into it.

Speaker ID	Utterance
1051336806	*but /you/ bug /me/*
1051336806	*and you hundred percent told peopel stfu.*

Table 3: Consecutive utterances made by the same speaker shall carry the same emotion.

4 Conclusion

In this work, we propose SA-BiLSTM to predict multiple emotions for given utterances in the dialogues. The proposed network is a self-attentive network built on top of BiLSTM. Our results evaluated on the validation set show that BiLSTM has better WA performance, while SA-BiLSTM is advantageous to BiLSTM in terms of UWA. According to the test results, SA-BiLSTM yields higher UWA scores for detecting the Neural emotion and the Joy emotions than the Sadness and the Anger ones. The bias may be caused by uneven training data distributions. We hope to improve our model by either incorporating more related data or retrieving more linguistic information.

Acknowledgment

This work was partially supported by the Research Grants Council of the Hong Kong Special Administrative Region, China (Project No. UGC/IDS14/16).

References

Dzmitry Bahdanau, Kyunghyun Cho, and Yoshua Bengio. 2014. Neural machine translation by jointly learning to align and translate. *CoRR*, abs/1409.0473.

Steven Bird. 2006. NLTK: the natural language toolkit. In *ACL 2006, 21st International Conference on Computational Linguistics and 44th Annual Meeting of the Association for Computational Linguistics, Proceedings of the Conference, Sydney, Australia, 17-21 July 2006*.

Sheng-Yeh Chen, Chao-Chun Hsu, Chuan-Chun Kuo, Ting-Hao Huang, and Lun-Wei Ku. 2018. Emotionlines: An emotion corpus of multi-party conversations. *CoRR*, abs/1802.08379.

Ronan Collobert and Jason Weston. 2008. A unified architecture for natural language processing: deep neural networks with multitask learning. In *Machine Learning, Proceedings of the Twenty-Fifth International Conference (ICML 2008), Helsinki, Finland, June 5-9, 2008*, pages 160–167.

Alexis Conneau, Douwe Kiela, Holger Schwenk, Loïc Barrault, and Antoine Bordes. 2017. Supervised learning of universal sentence representations from natural language inference data. In *Proceedings of the 2017 Conference on Empirical Methods in Natural Language Processing, EMNLP 2017, Copenhagen, Denmark, September 9-11, 2017*, pages 670–680.

Shalini Ghosh, Oriol Vinyals, Brian Strope, Scott Roy, Tom Dean, and Larry P. Heck. 2016. Contextual LSTM (CLSTM) models for large scale NLP tasks. *CoRR*, abs/1602.06291.

Sepp Hochreiter and Jürgen Schmidhuber. 1997. Long short-term memory. *Neural Computation*, 9(8):1735–1780.

Yanghoon Kim, Hwanhee Lee, and Kyomin Jung. 2018. Attnconvnet at semeval-2018 task 1: Attention-based convolutional neural networks for multi-label emotion classification. *CoRR*, abs/1804.00831.

Yoon Kim. 2014. Convolutional neural networks for sentence classification. In *Proceedings of the 2014 Conference on Empirical Methods in Natural Language Processing, EMNLP 2014, October 25-29, 2014, Doha, Qatar, A meeting of SIGDAT, a Special Interest Group of the ACL*, pages 1746–1751.

Diederik P. Kingma and Jimmy Ba. 2014. Adam: A method for stochastic optimization. *CoRR*, abs/1412.6980.

Zhouhan Lin, Minwei Feng, Cícero Nogueira dos Santos, Mo Yu, Bing Xiang, Bowen Zhou, and Yoshua Bengio. 2017. A structured self-attentive sentence embedding. *CoRR*, abs/1703.03130.

Pengfei Liu, Xipeng Qiu, and Xuanjing Huang. 2016. Recurrent neural network for text classification with multi-task learning. In *Proceedings of the Twenty-Fifth International Joint Conference on Artificial Intelligence, IJCAI 2016, New York, NY, USA, 9-15 July 2016*, pages 2873–2879.

Jeffrey Pennington, Richard Socher, and Christopher D. Manning. 2014. Glove: Global vectors for word representation. In *Proceedings of the 2014 Conference on Empirical Methods in Natural Language Processing, EMNLP 2014, October 25-29, 2014, Doha, Qatar, A meeting of SIGDAT, a Special Interest Group of the ACL*, pages 1532–1543.

Ashish Vaswani, Noam Shazeer, Niki Parmar, Jakob Uszkoreit, Llion Jones, Aidan N. Gomez, Lukasz Kaiser, and Illia Polosukhin. 2017. Attention is all you need. In *Advances in Neural Information Processing Systems 30: Annual Conference on Neural Information Processing Systems 2017, 4-9 December 2017, Long Beach, CA, USA*, pages 6000–6010.

EmotionX-AR: CNN-DCNN autoencoder based Emotion Classifier

Sopan Khosla

Big Data Experience Lab

Adobe Research, Bangalore, India

skhosla@adobe.com

Abstract

In this paper, we model emotions in EmotionLines dataset using a convolutional-deconvolutional autoencoder (CNN-DCNN) framework. We show that adding a joint reconstruction loss improves performance. Quantitative evaluation with jointly trained network, augmented with linguistic features, reports best accuracies for emotion prediction; namely joy, sadness, anger, and neutral emotion in text.

1 Introduction

Emotion recognition in content is an extensively studied area. It deals with associating words, phrases or documents with various categories of emotions. The importance of emotion analysis in human communication and interactions has been discussed by Picard (1997). Historically studied using multi-modal data, the study of human emotion from text and other published content has become an important topic in language understanding. Word correlation with social and psychological processes is discussed by Pennebaker (2011). Preotiuc-Pietro et al. (2017) studied personality and psycho-demographic preferences through Facebook and Twitter content. The analysis of emotion in interpersonal communication such as emails, chats and longer written articles is necessary for various applications including the study of consumer behavior and psychology, understanding audiences, and opinions in computational social science, and more recently for dialogue systems and conversational agents. This is an active research space today.

In contrast to sentiment analysis, emotion analysis in user generated content such as tweets (Dodds et al., 2011), blogs (Aman and Szpakowicz, 2007) and chats remains a space less trodden. The WASSA-2017 task on emotion intensity (Mohammad and Bravo-Marquez, 2017) aims at detecting the intensity of emotion felt by the author of a tweet. Whereas (Alm et al., 2005; Aman and Szpakowicz, 2007; Brooks et al., 2013; Neviarouskaya et al., 2009; Bollen et al., 2011) provide discrete binary labels to text instances for emotion classification. Typical discrete categories are a subset of those proposed by Ekman (Ekman, 1992) namely anger, joy, surprise, disgust, sadness, and fear.

Paper Structure: The remainder of the paper is organized as follows. We summarize the EmotionLines dataset in Section 2. Section 3 describes different parts of our system. We present our experiments in Section 4. Section 5 discusses the results of our final system submitted to the EmotionX challenge. Finally, we present conclusion and future directions in section 6.

2 Data

EmotionLines dataset contains dialogues from the Friends TV series and EmotionPush chat logs. Both Friends TV scripts and EmotionPush chat logs contain 1,000 dialogues split into training(720), development(80), and testing(200) set separately. In order to preserve completeness of any dialogue, the corpus was divided by the dialogues, not the utterances. Refer to Chen et al. (2018) for details on the dataset collection and construction.

The EmotionX task on EmotionLines dialogue dataset tries to capture the flow of emotion in a conversation. Given a dialogue, the task requires participants to determine the emotion of each utterance (in that dialogue) among four label candidates: joy, sadness, anger, and neutral.

Proceedings of the Sixth International Workshop on Natural Language Processing for Social Media , pages 37–44,
Melbourne, Australia, July 20, 2018. ©2018 Association for Computational Linguistics

3 System Description

In this section, we provide the technical details of our model.

3.1 Architecture Overview

We propose a joint learning framework for emotion detection built on a convolutional encoder (CNN). We introduce a joint learning objective where the network needs to learn the (1) utterance text (the data itself) and the (2) emotion information from the labeled data (EmotionLines) together. The CNN along with a deconvolutional decoder (DCNN) provides the mechanism for text reconstruction, i.e. to learn the text sequences. On the other hand, the learned encoding, augmented with linguistic features, acts as the input feature space for emotion detection.

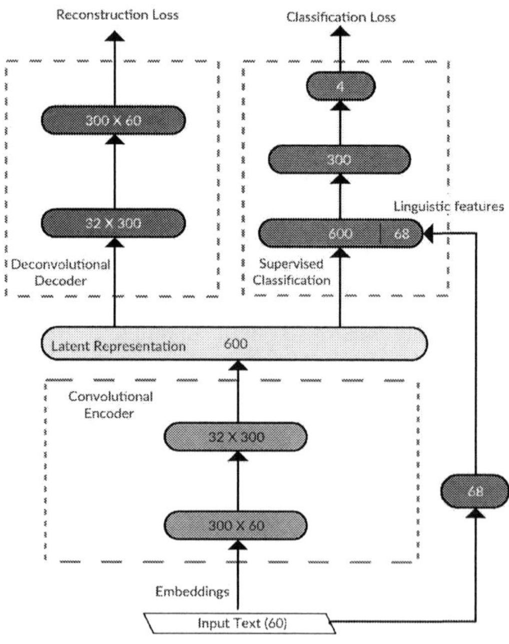

Figure 1: Architecture Overview

The architecture diagram is shown in figure 1. The network aims at emotion classification and in turn also learns the reconstruction objective. Key components of this approach are: **(1) Convolutional Autoencoder (CNN-DCNN), (2) Linguistic features, and (3) Joint-learning objective.**

Consider a text input d to the model. Each word w_d^t in d is embedded into a k-dimensional representation $e_t = \mathbf{E}[w_d^t]$ where $\mathbf{E}$ is a learned matrix. The embedding layer is passed through a CNN encoder to create a fixed-length vector $\mathbf{h_L}$ for the entire input text d. This latent representation, appended with linguistic features is then sent to a fully connected layer with a softmax classifier on top. Along with this, $\mathbf{h_L}$ is also fed to a deconvolutional decoder which attempts to reconstruct d from the latent vector. Therefore, the final loss function: $\alpha_{ae}L_{ae} + (1 - \alpha_{ae})L_c$ for the model is a combination of the classification error L_c and the reconstruction error L_{ae} explained in the following subsections.

3.2 CNN-DCNN Autoencoder

Zhang et al. (2017) introduce a sequence-to-sequence convolutional encoder followed by a deconvolutional decoder (CNN-DCNN) framework for learning latent representations from text data. Their proposed framework outperforms RNN-based networks for text reconstruction and semi-supervised classification tasks. We leverage their network in our work.

Convolutional Encoder. CNN with L layers, inspired from Radford et al. (2015) is used to encode the document into a latent representation vector, $\mathbf{h_L}$. Former $L - 1$ convolutional layers create a feature map which is fed into a fully-connected layer implemented as a convolutional layer. This final layer produces the latent representation $\mathbf{h_L}$ which acts as a fixed-dimensional summarization of the document.

Deconvolutional Decoder. We leverage the deconvolutional decoder introduced by Zhang el al. (2017) as is for our model. The reconstruction loss is defined as,

$$L_{ae} = \sum_{d \in D} \sum_t \log p(\hat{w}_d^t = w_d^t), \quad (1)$$

where D is the set of observed sentences. w_d^t and $\hat{w}_d^t$ correspond to the words in the input and output sequences respectively.

3.3 Linguistic Features

Here, we explain the various linguistic features used in our network. Inspired from Chhaya et al, (2018), we use 68 linguistic features further divided into 4 sub-groups: Lexical, Syntactic, Derived and Affect-based. The lexical and syntactic features include features such as 'averageNumberofWords per sentence' and 'number of capitalizations'. Features that can help quantify readability of text are the part of derived features.

Thus, this set contains features like Hedges, Contractions, and Readability scores. The fourth group of features are the Affect–related features. These features are lexica–based and quantify the amount of affective content present in the text. All features used by Pavlick et al. (2016) for formality detection and by Danescu et al. (2013) for politeness detection are included in our analysis. We use Stanford CoreNLP[1] and TextBlob[2] feature extraction and pre-processing.

Lexical and Syntactic Features: The lexical features capture various counts associated with the content like '#Question Marks', 'Average Word Length' etc. Syntactic features include NER–based features, Number of blank lines, and text density which is defined as follows:

$$\rho = \frac{\#(sentences)}{1 + \#(lines)}$$

where ρ is the text density, $\#(sentences)$ denotes number of sentences in the text content and $\#(lines)$ number of lines including blank lines in the text message. Prior art in NLP extensively relies on these features for their analysis.

Derived: Readability Features: The derived features capture information such as readability of text, existence of hedges, subjectivity, contractions and sign–offs. Subjectivity, contractions and hedges are based on the TextBlob implementation. Readability is measured based on Flesh–Kincaid readability score. This score is a measure of ease of reading of given piece of text. We use the textstat package[3] in Python for implementation.

Psycholinguistic Features: The affect features used in our analysis include:

1. **Valence-Arousal-Dominance (VAD) Model** (Mehrabian, 1980): We use the Warriner's lexicon (Warriner et al., 2013) for these features. This lexicon contains real-valued scores for Valence, Arousal, and Dominance (VAD) on a scale of 1 9 each for 13915 English words. 1, 5, 9 correspond to the low, moderate (i.e. neutral), and high values for each dimension respectively.

2. **Ekman's Emotions (Ekman, 1992):** Ekman introdcued six fundamental emotions namely anger, joy, surprise, disgust, sadness, and fear. In this work, we use the NRC lexicon (EMOLEX) (Mohammad et al., 2013) which provides a measure for the existence of the emotion as well as the intensity of the detected emotion on word level.

3. **PERMA Model (Seligman, 2011):** The PERMA model is a scale to measure positivity and well–being in humans (Seligman, 2011). This model defines the 5 dimensions: Positive Emotions, Engagement, Relationships, Meaning, and Accomplishments as quantifiers and indicators of positivity and well–being. Schwartz et al. (Schwartz et al., 2013) published a PERMA lexicon. We use this lexicon in our work.

Formality Lists:We use the formality list, provided by Brooke et al. (2010), for our experiments. It contains a set of words usually used to express formality or informality in text.

3.4 Supervised Classification

Traditional affective language studies focus on analyzing features including lexical (Pennebaker et al., 2001), syntactic, and psycholinguistic features to detect emotions. We augment the latent vector produced by CNN encoder with the set of linguistic features (Section 3.3) to capture emotions.

Let $\boldsymbol{h}'$ denote the representation vector for linguistic features extracted from the input data d. $\boldsymbol{h}'$ is normalized and concatenated with $\boldsymbol{h_L}$ to derive $\boldsymbol{h}'' = \boldsymbol{h_L} \frown \boldsymbol{h}'$. $\boldsymbol{h}''$, producing a probability p_n for each neuron in the softmax layer, where y_n denotes the ground-truth for corresponding class n.

We use cross-entropy based classwise loss as given below:

$$loss_n = -\Big[y_n \log(p_n) + (1 - y_n) \log(1 - p_n) \Big]$$

Since, EmotionLines suffers from class imbalance, we give higher weight (w_n) to the losses incurred on data samples of minority classes.

$$\frac{1}{w_n} = \frac{a_n}{\sum_{i=1}^{N} a_i}$$

where a_n denote the number of samples of class n in the training set. Finally, we use a weighted

---

[1] https://stanfordnlp.github.io/CoreNLP/
[2] https://textblob.readthedocs.io/en/dev/
[3] https://pypi.python.org/pypi/textstat/0.1.6

Features	Feature list
Lexical	Average Word Length, Average Words per Sentence, # of Upper Case Words, # Ellipses, # Exclamation marks, # Question Mark, # Multiple Question Marks, # Words, # Lower Case words, First word upper case, # NonAlphaChars, # Punctuation Chars
Syntactic	# BlankLines, NER-Person, NER-Location, NER-PersonLength, NER-Organization, TextDensity
Derived	# Contractions, ReadabilityScore- FKgrade, FirstPerson, Hedge, Subjectivity, Sentiment, ThirdPerson, SignOff
Psycholingistic Features	ANEW-arousal, ANEW-dominance, ANEW-valence, EmolexIntensity-anger, EmolexIntensity-fear, EmolexIntensity-joy, EmolexIntensity-sadness, Emolex-anger, Emolex-anticipation, Emolex-disgust, Emolex-fear, Emolex-joy, Emolex-negative, Emolex-positive, Emolex-sadness, Emolex-surprise, Emolex-trust, Perma-NEG-A, Perma-NEG-E, Perma-NEG-M, Perma-NEG-P, Perma-NEG-R, Perma-POS-A, Perma-POS-E, Perma-POS-M, Perma-POS-P, Perma-POS-R
Formal Words	formal-words, informal-words (Brooke et al., 2010)

Table 1: Summary of feature groups used in our model.

Friends TV Series Script	WA	UWA	Joy	Sad	Ang	Neu
CNN + MLP (S)	67.67	57.61	**66.67**	38.70	38.82	**76.58**
S + Joint Learning (J)	67.40	58.47	63.41	45.16	38.82	76.17
S + Linguistic Features (L)	65.30	59.48	**66.67**	43.55	**47.06**	70.88
S + J + L	60.97	59.39	59.35	**58.06**	44.71	64.56

EmotionPush Chat Logs	WA	UWA	Joy	Sad	Ang	Neu
CNN + MLP (S)	68.89	59.22	69.37	**76.31**	22.22	68.97
S + Joint Learning (J)	70.44	59.58	68.75	**76.31**	22.22	**71.03**
S + Linguistic Features (L)	67.54	64.03	70.00	63.16	**55.56**	67.39
S + J + L	65.69	65.08	**71.88**	68.42	**55.56**	64.48

Table 2: Weighted (WA) and Unweighted (UWA) accuracies(%) on Friends and EmotionPush validation sets provided by the challenge authors. **S**: Supervised learning using CNN encoder trained on labeled data only, **J**: Joint learning with reconstruction task using DCNN decoder, **L**: Linguistic features.

cross entropy loss defined by

$$L_c = -\frac{1}{N} \sum_{n=1}^{N} w_n * loss_n \qquad (2)$$

Table 1 provides a summary of the features considered. Ngrams and other semantic features are ignored as they introduce domain-specific biases. Word-embeddings are treated separately and considered as raw features to train a supervised model.

3.5 Joint learning

The CNN-DCNN network learns the text information i.e. sequences, the linguistic features learn the emotional aspect. Joint learning introduces the mechanism to learn shared representations during the network training. We implement joint learning using simultaneous optimization for both sequence reconstruction (CNN-DCNN) and emotion detection (linguistic features). The combined loss function is given by,

$$L = \alpha_{ae} L_{ae} + (1 - \alpha_{ae}) L_c. \qquad (3)$$

where α_{ae} is a balancing hyperparameter with $0 \leq \alpha_{ae} \leq 1$. Higher the value of α_{ae}, higher is the importance given to the reconstruction loss L_{ae} while training and vice versa.

Friends	WA	UWA	Joy	Sad	Ang	Neu
S	64.90	59.09	69.10	53.22	45.88	68.24
S + J	69.54	60.54	**71.54**	51.67	45.88	**75.20**
S + L	62.78	59.16	62.60	**54.10**	56.47	64.75
S + J + L	65.83	60.48	68.29	48.33	**58.82**	68.44

EmPush	WA	UWA	Joy	Sad	Ang	Neu
S	68.89	64.62	80.62	52.63	**66.67**	58.54
S + J	70.44	60.53	**85.00**	58.97	33.33	63.27
S + L	67.54	62.95	76.87	56.41	44.44	**72.60**
S + J + L	65.69	64.89	75.62	**63.16**	55.56	65.21

Table 3: Accuracy(%) for models trained on Friends + EmotionPush data, tested on individual validation sets.

4 Experiments

In this section, we show the experimental evaluation of our system on the EmotionLines dataset.

4.1 Experimental Setup

CNN encoder with MLP Classifier: We use 300-dimensional pre-trained glove word-embeddings (Pennington et al., 2014) as input to the model. The encoder contains two convolutional layers. Size of the latent representation is set to 600. The MLP classifier contains one fully-connected layer followed by a softmax layer.

Joint Training: We set $\alpha_{ae} = 0.5$ as this gives equal importance to both objectives and reports best results.

Linguistic Features: We concatenate a full set of 68 linguistic features with the latent representation for emotion detection.

Friends	UWA	Joy	Sad	Ang	Neu
Our Model	**62.5**	**71.1**	**55.3**	**55.3**	68.3
Highest	62.5	71.1	55.3	55.3	**99.5**

EmPush	UWA	Joy	Sad	Ang	Neu
Our Model	**62.5**	**76.0**	51.7	**45.9**	76.3
Highest	62.5	76.0	**54.0**	45.9	**99.0**

Table 4: Results on the EmotionX challenge test sets for Friends and EmotionPush datasets. Accuracy(%) rounded off to one decimal point.

4.2 Results

Table 2 shows the results for models trained on individual training sets using our weighted loss function. The performance is evaluated using both, the weighted accuracy (WA) and the unweighted accuracy (UWA), as defined by the challenge authors (Chen et al., 2018).

$$WA = \sum_{c \in C} p_c a_c \qquad (4)$$

$$UWA = \frac{1}{|C|} \sum_{c \in C} a_c \qquad (5)$$

where a_c denotes the accuracy of emotion class c and p_c denotes the percentage of utterances in emotion class c.

Adding a reconstruction loss with classification loss improves performance. We attribute this to improved generalizability provided by a semi-supervised loss. Concatenating linguistic features improves minority class accuracies for both Friends TV dialogues and EmotionPush chats. The improvements due to joint loss and linguistic features are more significant for EmotionPush chat log dataset. Accuracies of majority class (Neutral) take a considerable hit with the addition of **J** and **L** for both datasets, whereas minority emotions like Sadness and Anger consistently benefit from addition of linguistic features.

Table 3 contains results for models trained on both Friends and EmotionPush training data. Increase in training data, even though from a different domain, improves performance for Joy and Anger emotions. Accuracy on sadness dips significantly for EmotionPush. Overall WA and UWA also increase slightly for Friends dataset.

5 EmotionX Submission and Analysis

We implement an ensemble of the four model variants trained on the Friends + EmotionPush data as our final submission for the EmotionX challenge. We arrive at the final class predictions using the algorithm explained in Algorithm 1. For each test

---

Algorithm 1 Ensemble Algorithm

```
 1: procedure FILTER(p_x, threshold)
 2:     candidates ← []
 3:     for p ∈ p_x do                                              ▷ For each base model
 4:         if max(p) > threshold then
 5:             candidates.add(arg max(p)))
 6:         end if
 7:     end for
 8:     return candidates
 9: end procedure
10:
11: procedure ENSEMBLE(data, p_softmax)   ▷ p_softmax.shape = (#test samples, #models, #classes)
12:     ensemble_pred ← []
13:     for x ∈ data do
14:         candidate_classes ← FILTER(p_softmax[x], 0.75)                  ▷ High Confidence
15:         if len(candidate_classes) > 0 then
16:             ensemble_pred.add(most_common(candidates))
17:         else
18:             candidate_classes ← FILTER(p_softmax[x], 0.50)             ▷ Moderate Confidence
19:             if len(candidate_classes) > 0 then
20:                 ensemble_pred.add(most_common(candidate_classes)))
21:             else
22:                 candidate_classes ← FILTER(p_softmax[x], 0.00)          ▷ Low Confidence
23:                 ensemble_pred.add(most_common(candidate_classes))
24:             end if
25:         end if
26:     end for
27:     return ensemble_predictions
28: end procedure
```

---

sample, we find models for which the maximum output probability associated with a class is greater than a threshold of 0.75 (High Confidence). Predictions from this subset are considered as the candidate high confidence classes. The most common class in this subset is taken as the final prediction for EmotionX submission. If the subset is empty, a similar approach is followed but with a reduced threshold of 0.50 (Moderate Confidence). Predictions for samples which do not satisfy any of the above thresholds are termed as Low Confidence Predictions.

The results on the test-set for both datasets are shown in Table 4. Comparison with the best results in each class shows that for Friends dataset, our model tops for all emotions except Neutral. Whereas, for the EmotionPush dataset, we perform well on Joy and Anger. Our model had the best unweighted accuracy (UWA) for both datasets in the EmotionX challenge.

Text	Prediction	Label
Come on, Lydia, you can do it.	Neutral	Neutral
Push!	Anger	**Joy**
Push 'em out, push 'em out, harder, harder.	Anger	**Joy**
Push 'em out, push 'em out, way out!	Anger	**Joy**
Let's get that ball and really move, hey, hey, ho, ho.	Joy	Joy
Let's– I was just–yeah, right.	Joy	Joy
Push!	Anger	**Joy**
Push!	Anger	**Joy**

Table 5: An example dialogue from Friends dataset with corresponding predictions and labels.

5.1 Error Analysis

Our model does not explicitly import contextual information from other utterances in the conversation. Therefore, quite expectedly, we found that most of the utterances misclassified by our model occur in dialogues where the current utterance does not exhibit the emotion it is tagged with.

Another set of errors occur where the whole conversation is not able to explain the respective emotions of each utterance. Table 5 shows an example conversation where it might be difficult for even a human to classify the utterances without the associated multi-modal cues.

6 Conclusion and Future Work

We propose a CNN-DCNN autoencoder based approach for emotion detection on EmotionLines dataset. We show that addition of a semi-supervised loss improves performance. We propose multiple linguistic features which are concatenated to the latent encoded representation for classification. The results show that our model detects emotions successfully. The network, using a weighted classification loss function, tries to handle the class imbalance in the dataset.

In future, we plan to include results of modeling emotion on the whole dialog using an LSTM layer over our network. We would experiment with concatenating subsets of linguistic features to better estimate the contribution of each feature group. We also plan to use data-augmentation techniques such as backtranslation and word substitution using Wordnet and word-embeddings in order to handle class-imbalance in the dataset.

References

Cecilia Ovesdotter Alm, Dan Roth, and Richard Sproat. 2005. Emotions from text: machine learning for text-based emotion prediction. In *Proceedings of the conference on human language technology and empirical methods in natural language processing*. Association for Computational Linguistics, pages 579–586.

Saima Aman and Stan Szpakowicz. 2007. Identifying expressions of emotion in text. In *International Conference on Text, Speech and Dialogue*. Springer, pages 196–205.

Piotr Bojanowski, Edouard Grave, Armand Joulin, and Tomas Mikolov. 2016. Enriching word vectors with subword information. *CoRR* abs/1607.04606. http://arxiv.org/abs/1607.04606.

Johan Bollen, Huina Mao, and Alberto Pepe. 2011. Modeling public mood and emotion: Twitter sentiment and socio-economic phenomena. *Icwsm* 11:450–453.

Julian Brooke, Tong Wang, and Graeme Hirst. 2010. Automatic acquisition of lexical formality. In *Proceedings of the 23rd International Conference on Computational Linguistics: Posters*. Association for Computational Linguistics, pages 90–98.

Michael Brooks, Katie Kuksenok, Megan K Torkildson, Daniel Perry, John J Robinson, Taylor J Scott, Ona Anicello, Ariana Zukowski, Paul Harris, and Cecilia R Aragon. 2013. Statistical affect detection in collaborative chat. In *Proceedings of the 2013 conference on Computer supported cooperative work*. ACM, pages 317–328.

Sheng-Yeh Chen, Chao-Chun Hsu, Chuan-Chun Kuo, Lun-Wei Ku, et al. 2018. Emotionlines: An emotion corpus of multi-party conversations. *arXiv preprint arXiv:1802.08379* .

Niyati Chhaya, Kushal Chawla, Tanya Goyal, Projjal Chanda, and Jaya Singh. 2018. Frustrated, polite or formal: Quantifying feelings and tone in emails. In *Second Workshop on Computational Modeling of Peoples Opinions, Personality, and Emotions in Social Media, NAACL HLT* .

Cristian Danescu-Niculescu-Mizil, Moritz Sudhof, Dan Jurafsky, Jure Leskovec, and Christopher Potts. 2013. A computational approach to politeness with application to social factors. *arXiv preprint arXiv:1306.6078* .

Peter Sheridan Dodds, Kameron Decker Harris, Isabel M Kloumann, Catherine A Bliss, and Christopher M Danforth. 2011. Temporal patterns of happiness and information in a global social network: Hedonometrics and twitter. *PloS one* 6(12):e26752.

Paul Ekman. 1992. An argument for basic emotions. *Cognition & Emotion* 6(3-4):169–200.

Albert Mehrabian. 1980. Basic dimensions for a general psychological theory implications for personality, social, environmental, and developmental studies .

Saif M Mohammad and Felipe Bravo-Marquez. 2017. Wassa-2017 shared task on emotion intensity. *arXiv preprint arXiv:1708.03700* .

Saif M Mohammad, Svetlana Kiritchenko, and Xiaodan Zhu. 2013. Nrc-canada: Building the state-of-the-art in sentiment analysis of tweets. *arXiv preprint arXiv:1308.6242* .

Alena Neviarouskaya, Helmut Prendinger, and Mitsuru Ishizuka. 2009. Compositionality principle in recognition of fine-grained emotions from text. In *ICWSM* .

Ellie Pavlick and Joel Tetreault. 2016. An empirical analysis of formality in online communication. *Transactions of the Association for Computational Linguistics* 4:61–74.

James W Pennebaker, Martha E Francis, and Roger J Booth. 2001. Linguistic inquiry and word count: Liwc 2001. *Mahway: Lawrence Erlbaum Associates* 71:2001.

J.W. Pennebaker. 2011. *The Secret Life of Pronouns: What Our Words Say About Us*. Bloomsbury USA. https://books.google.com/books?id=Avz4rthHySEC.

Jeffrey Pennington, Richard Socher, and Christopher Manning. 2014. Glove: Global vectors for word representation. In *Proceedings of the 2014 conference on empirical methods in natural language processing (EMNLP)*. pages 1532–1543.

Rosalind W. Picard. 1997. *Affective Computing*. MIT Press, Cambridge, MA, USA.

Daniel Preotiuc-Pietro, Ye Liu, Daniel J. Hopkins, and Lyle Ungar. 2017. Personality Driven Differences in Paraphrase Preference. In *Proceedings of the Workshop on Natural Language Processing and Computational Social Science (NLP+CSS)*. ACL.

Alec Radford, Luke Metz, and Soumith Chintala. 2015. Unsupervised representation learning with deep convolutional generative adversarial networks. *arXiv preprint arXiv:1511.06434* .

Sascha Rothe, Sebastian Ebert, and Hinrich Schütze. 2016. Ultradense word embeddings by orthogonal transformation. *CoRR* abs/1602.07572. http://arxiv.org/abs/1602.07572.

H Andrew Schwartz, Johannes C Eichstaedt, Margaret L Kern, Lukasz Dziurzynski, Stephanie M Ramones, Megha Agrawal, Achal Shah, Michal Kosinski, David Stillwell, Martin EP Seligman, et al. 2013. Personality, gender, and age in the language of social media: The open-vocabulary approach. *PloS one* 8(9):e73791.

João Sedoc, Jean Gallier, Lyle H. Ungar, and Dean P. Foster. 2016. Semantic word clusters using signed normalized graph cuts. *CoRR* abs/1601.05403. http://arxiv.org/abs/1601.05403.

Martin EP Seligman. 2011. Flourish: a visionary new understanding of happiness and well-being. *Policy* 27(3):60–1.

Ivan Vulic, Nikola Mrksic, Roi Reichart, Diarmuid Ó Séaghdha, Steve J. Young, and Anna Korhonen. 2017. Morph-fitting: Fine-tuning word vector spaces with simple language-specific rules. *CoRR* abs/1706.00377. http://arxiv.org/abs/1706.00377.

Amy Beth Warriner, Victor Kuperman, and Marc Brysbaert. 2013. Norms of valence, arousal, and dominance for 13,915 english lemmas. *Behavior Research Methods* 45(4):1191–1207.

Yizhe Zhang, Dinghan Shen, Guoyin Wang, Zhe Gan, Ricardo Henao, and Lawrence Carin. 2017. Deconvolutional paragraph representation learning. *CoRR* abs/1708.04729. http://arxiv.org/abs/1708.04729.

EmotionX-SmartDubai_NLP: Detecting User Emotions In Social Media Text

Rahul Venkatesh Kumar, Shahram Rahmanian, Hessa Albalooshi
Smart Services Department
Smart Dubai Government Establishment
Dubai, United Arab Emirates

Abstract

This paper describes the working note on "EmotionX" shared task. It is hosted by SocialNLP 2018. The objective of this task is to detect the emotions, based on each speaker's utterances that are in English. Taking this as multiclass text classification problem, we have experimented to develop a model to classify the target class. The primary challenge in this task is to detect the emotions in short messages, communicated through social media. This paper describes the participation of SmartDubai_NLP team in EmotionX shared task and our investigation to detect the emotions from utterance using Neural networks and Natural language understanding.

1 Introduction

Emotions play a vital part in communication when people interact between each other. The exchange of emotions through text message and blog post in an informal way of writing is a bigger challenge for any machine to understand. Detecting emotions from text is widely used recently in the fields of neuroscience and cognitive services to analyze the consumer behaviors. [6] Emotion detection task is similar to analyzing the sentiment in a text. In this task we aim to detect and recognize types of feelings through the utterance such as "Neutral" "Joy" "Sadness" and "Anger". These four emotions types are related to the facial expression analysis in image recognition field. One of the most colossal challenges in determining emotion is the context dependence of emotions within the text [6]. Another challenge is linguistic co-reference, word sense disambiguation and ambiguity. Here, we describe the method and ideology of detecting the emotion from the text. The regular text classification works by stacking the text representations followed by the learned features. By considering the above discussion, our research model is given in Figure 1.

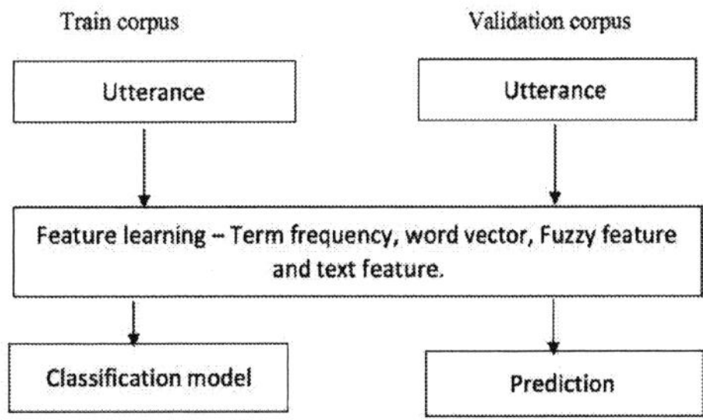

Figure 1: Experimental model

The description of task approach is explained in detail in the following sections 2. Task description, Section 3. Corpus Description, Section 4. Corpus Statistics, Section 5. Methodology Section 6. Feature Engineering, Section 7. Experiment, Section 8. Result Analysis and 9. Error Analysis and Conclusion.

2 Task Description

The given dataset consists of "Speaker", "Utterance" and "Emotion". Utterance text tagged with the emotion information, the objective is to detect the emotion information for the utterance in the validation set. The equation tag ϵ {Neutral, Joy, Sadness, Anger} and (n) represent the total number of target class in the dataset.

$$train\_corpus = \left\{ \left(utterance_1, target_1 \right), \left(utterance_2, target_2 \right), ..., \left(utterance_n, target_n \right) \right\} (1)$$

$$validation\_corpus = \left\{ utterance_1, utterance_2, ..., utterance_n \right\} (2)$$

3 Corpus Description

Corpus is provided by Emotion X SocialNLP 2018 shared task organizers. Training set and validation set both are in the Json format. Input utterance is annotated with target class in the training set. The training data contains total

Proceedings of the Sixth International Workshop on Natural Language Processing for Social Media , pages 45–49,
Melbourne, Australia, July 20, 2018. ©2018 Association for Computational Linguistics

9113 utterance with 4 emotion categories and validation and test data contains 1023 and 5573

utterances without target class. The sample training and validation set are mentioned in table 1.

Emotion	Utterance
neutral	If I do have it, I never used it
joy	Oh cool
sadness	Maybe your love for me doesn't fly
anger	Can't you just not put me in such situations in front of people

Table 1: Training data sample

4   Corpus Statistics

The dataset is primarily the conversation between two speakers. In training set most belongs to neutral utterance (78 percentage) and least belongs to anger utterance (1 percentage) Table 2. In training and test set utterance is mixed with digits, punctuations, and emoji's. Quality of utterance are most challenging task here because of social media content user own text scripts. In training data, we see that longer sentences belong to the neutral category and shorter sentences belong to the anger category. Using Term frequency method, we can see that there are larger number of numeric values and internet slang term like 'lol','haha' and 'idk' are used in the utterances. The utterance word count and target correlation are showed in the figure 2 using violin plot.

	neutral	Joy	sadness	anger
Training Set Size	7148	1482	389	94
Validation Set Size	825	160	38	9

Table 2: Corpus Count

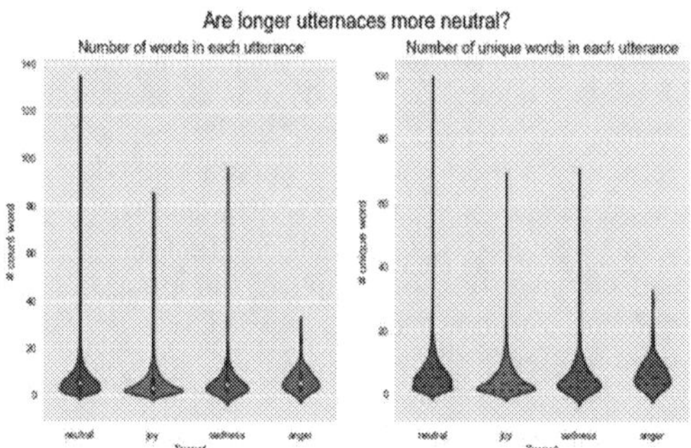

Figure 2: Word count vs Target

5   Methodology

The figure 3 gives a picture of the architecture that we have currently implemented for this task. We are primarily focused on data pre-processing to improve the quality of utterances and also enhance feature representations. We started our approach with simple term frequency based on CNN+BiLSTM; the same methods are discussed next.

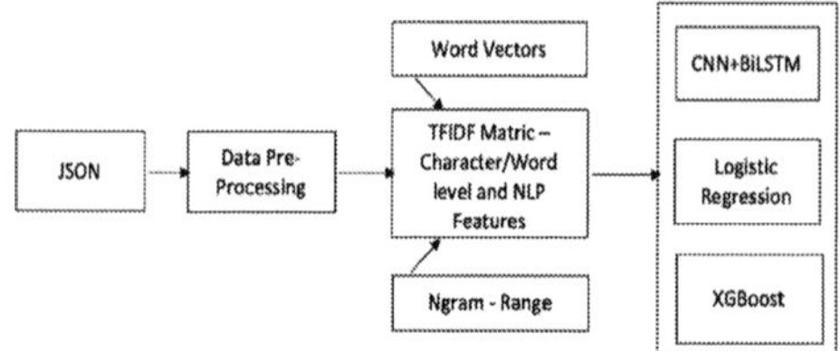

Figure 3: Architecture of our approach

6 Feature Engineering

We have improved our model accuracy on each step of stacking and modifying the features. Our whole approach is based on the architecture model figure 3. Below are the steps followed before building the model. Performance improved after data cleansing.

6.1 Data Normalization

In data normalization step we have mainly focused on cleaning the utterance to improve the performance of the model. We have created the custom list of words to replace the internet slang tokens with proper words and the same method is followed for replacing the emoji's in utterances with corresponding meaning. In addition to this, shorthand's text is replaced with proper abbreviation and mutli spaces with single space. Some of the speakers have empty utterance we have replaced the empty utterance with word "empty line". Sample data set is show in the table 3.

Utterance Before Preprocessing	Utterance After Preprocessing
lol	
	lots of laughs
do you even have the page liked? :)	do you even have the page liked? smile
how long you been working? :-(	how long you been working? sad
i can't understand all too smart hahahahaha	i cannot understand all too smart smile

Table 3: Utterance after cleaning

6.2 Count Based model

Our first approach is the Concatenates of Word level ngram Term Frequency Inverse Document Frequency(TFIDF) and Character level ngram Term Frequency Inverse Document Frequency(TFIDF) as single feature using sklearn FeatureUnion.

6.3 NLP Features

As a part of feature engineering, we have added hand craft features from the utterances to improve our model. The sample of the features are shown in below points.

- Length of each utterance
- Number of words in each utterance
- Number of stop words in each utterance
- Percentage of unique words each
- Sentiment polarity of each utterance

7 Experiment

As a part of experiment analysis, we ran few best algorithms like Logistic regression, Support Vector with 'rbf' kernel, Multinomial Navi Bayes. In deep learning we tried with Convolutional Neural Network - Bilateral (Long Short-Term Memory) and Convolutional Neural Network - Long Short-Term Memory(LSTM) with fastText word vector. The main advantage of using neural network is that the necessity of heavy lifting on the feature engineering side is minimum. Training set is split into training and validation data with ration 0.2 in below approaches.

(1) The word count based approach is taken as baseline approach, for this we have considered the Concatenates Word level and Character level matrix as feature using Logistic regression with accuracy of 91%. We have used ngram_range = 1,1 in Word level and ngram_range = 1,3.

(2) The second approach we have used is the combination of Word and Character level ngram Term Frequency Inverse Document Frequency(TFIDF) with handcrafted NLP features using GridSearchCV on Logistic regression with accuracy of 77% and XGBClassifier with accuracy of 85%.

(3) The third approach is using neural networks with custom hyper parameters. After prepressing each utterance is given as an input to the network. CNN+BiLSTM – accuracy of 84%. CNN+LSTM with fast Text word vector – accuracy of 86%.

Result of each model run is evaluated using precision, recall, accuracy and F1 score. The result is mentioned in the table 5.

Model	Accuracy %	Precision	Recall	F1-score
Logistic Regression (Char+Word Tfidf)	0.91	0.92	0.92	0.92
Multinomial Naive Bayes (Char+Word Tfidf)	0.85	0.83	0.83	0.78
Xgboost (TFIDF+NLP Features)	0.85	0.89	0.90	0.89
CNN+BiLSTM	0.84.9	0.80	0.85	0.82
CNN+LSTM(fastText wordvector)	0.85.7	0.81	0.86	0.83

Table :5 Cross validation results with different classifiers

8 Result Analysis

The combined feature of Character level with trigram and word level ngram using logistic regression model achieved overall 91.83% accuracy for this multiclass text classification, followed by CNN-LSTM. To classify the text properly we have used custom parameters in term frequency-inverse document frequency and logistic regression. Due to imbalanced data set and social media format contents we have concentrated more on the data preparation and it help us to improved our overall accuracy and our model performance. Our approach for detecting the emotion in the text has been evaluated based on the unweighted accuracy and class wise metrics precision, recall and F1 measure scores are mentioned in the table 6.

Target Class	Precision %	Recall %	F1-score %
neutral	0.84	0.94	0.89
joy	0.82	0.77	0.79
sadness	0.94	0.96	0.95
anger	0.82	0.80	0.81
Average %	0.92	0.92	0.92

Table :6 Target wise performance analysis

We have obtained an overall accuracy of 91.83% using Stacked Tf-idf features logistic regression-based approach for EmotionX" shared task SocialNLP 2018 - Detecting User Emotions in Social Media Text.

8.1 Evaluation Result

The test data contains two files Emotion push and Friends utterances with 50571 unlabeled data and submission of labeled was evaluated by the task organizer final ranking is based on the Unweighted Accuracy mentioned on the below table 7. It was quite disappointment our model didn't perform well on the test data.

Test data	Unweighted Accuracy
Emotion Push	26.55
Friends	25.52

9 Error Analysis and Conclusion

In this paper, a supervised system for we have presented an approach to detect the emotion in speaker utterances which is in social media format. Our experimented methodology, Charterer and Word level ngram stacked feature extracted from utterances. Then the logistic regression with custom parameters is trained using extracted features. Our system is evaluated using the test utterances given EmotionX shared task organizers. We have obtained an overall accuracy of 91.83% in the training set but fails to capture generalized features and performs poorly on the test set. The major drawback is imbalanced data for training set. Another issue dealing with large amount internet slang in dataset. The system could further have improved by replacing the internet slang with proper lexical and experiment with different techniques used on the supervised approach in Machine learning.

ACKNOWLEDGMENTS

We are thankful to the Smart Dubai Government Establishment authorities for providing the support and infrastructure facilities to pursing the work done for this research project.

References

[1] KP Soman Rahul Venkatesh Kumar, Anand Kumar M,AmritaCEN_NLP@ FIRE 2015 Language Identification for Indian Languages in Social Media Text.

[2] Rongyu Li, Feng Zhou, Jing Wang, Xiaojian Yang, "Application of improved multiple convolution neural network in emotion polarity classification model", Chinese Automation Congress (CAC) 2017, pp. 644-649, 2017.

[3] Yuanye He,Liang-Chih Yu1,K.Robert Lai and Weiyi Liu4YZU-NLP at EmoInt-2017:Determining.

[4] Barathi Ganesh HB, Reshma U, Anand Kumar M and Soman KP,Representation of Target Classes for Text Classification.

[5] Vivek Vinayan, Naveen J R, Harikrishnan NB, Anand Kumar M and Soman KP,AmritaNLP@PAN-RusProfiling : Author Profiling using Machine Learning Techniques.

[6] Emotion Detection and Recognition from Text Using Deep Learning by CY Yam.

[7] Text Based Emotion Recognition: A Survey by Chetan R Chopade.

EmotionX-Area66: Predicting Emotions in Dialogues using Hierarchical Attention Network with Sequence Labeling

Rohit Saxena
TCS Research
rohit.saxena2@tcs.com

Savita Bhat
TCS Research
savita.bhat@tcs.com

Niranjan Pedanekar
TCS Research
n.pedanekar@tcs.com

Abstract

This paper presents our system submitted to the EmotionX challenge. It is an emotion detection task on dialogues in the EmotionLines dataset. We formulate this as a hierarchical network where network learns data representation at both utterance level and dialogue level. Our model is inspired by Hierarchical Attention network (HAN) and uses pre-trained word embeddings as features. We formulate emotion detection in dialogues as a sequence labeling problem to capture the dependencies among labels. We report the performance accuracy for four emotions (*anger, joy, neutral* and *sadness*). The model achieved unweighted accuracy of 55.38% on *Friends* test dataset and 56.73% on *EmotionPush* test dataset. We report an improvement of 22.51% in *Friends* dataset and 36.04% in *EmotionPush* dataset over baseline results.

1 Introduction

Emotion detection and classification constitutes a significant part of research in the area of natural language processing (NLP). The research aims to detect presence of an emotion in a text snippet and correctly categorize the same. The emotions are typically classified using categories proposed by (Ekman et al., 1987), namely *anger, disgust, fear, joy, sadness, surprise*. Significant amount of research has been dedicated to emotion classification in variety of texts like news and news headlines (Strapparava and Mihalcea, 2008; Staiano and Guerini, 2014), blogposts (Mishne, 2005), fiction (Mohammad, 2012b).

With the advent of social media and dialogue systems like personal assistants and chatbots,

Speaker	Utterance	Emotion
Joey	Whoa-whoa, Treeger made you cry?	surprise
Rachel	Yes! And he said really mean things that were only partly true.	sadness
Joey	I'm gonna go down there and teach that guy a lesson.	anger
Monica	Joey, please don't do that. I think it's best that we just forget about it.	fear
Rachel	That's easy for you to say, you weren't almost just killed.	anger
Joey	All right that's it, school is in session!	neutral

Table 1: Example of a dialogue from *Friends* dataset

emotion analysis of short texts has garnered a lot of attention. Short texts are defined as small text chunks in the form of tweets, messenger conversations, social network posts, conversational dialogues etc. Unlike large documents, these texts have unique set of characteristics such as informal language, incomplete sentences, use of emoticons. Different approaches for emotion detection in short texts are proposed in (Krcadinac et al., 2013) for instant messages, (Mohammad, 2012a) and (Wang et al., 2012) for *Twitter* and (Preotiuc-Pietro et al., 2016) for status updates in *Facebook*.

Conversational short texts consist of dialogues between two or more entities. A dialogue naturally has a hierarchical structure, with words contributing to an utterance and a set of utterances contributing to a dialogue (Kumar et al., 2017). Table 1 shows an example of a dialogue which consists of 6 utterances with corresponding speakers

Proceedings of the Sixth International Workshop on Natural Language Processing for Social Media , pages 50–55,
Melbourne, Australia, July 20, 2018. ©2018 Association for Computational Linguistics

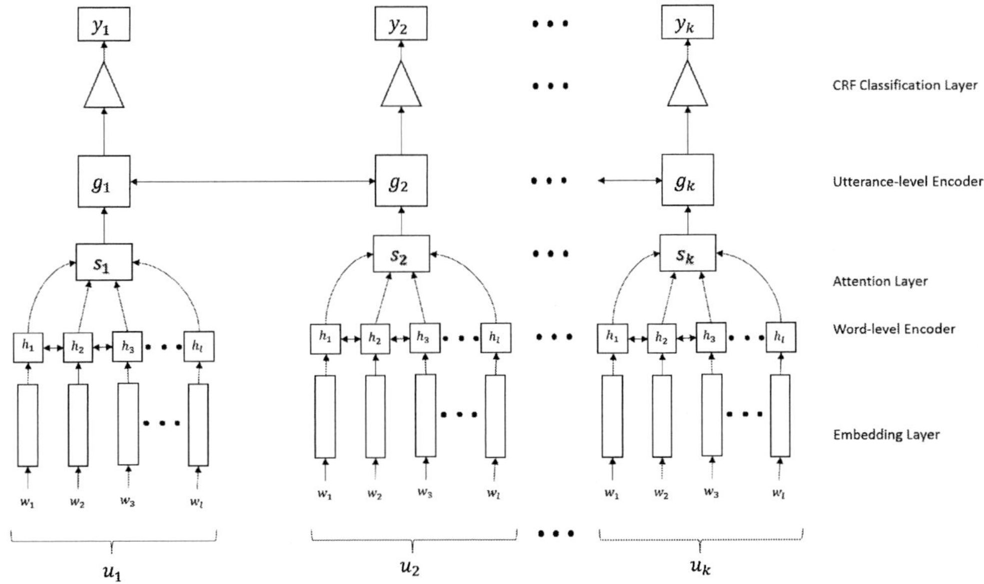

Figure 1: An illustration of proposed Hierarchical Attention Network

and emotions. In these dialogues, context builds as the dialogue progresses. There is a dependency between consecutive utterances and hence the classification of such utterances can be treated as a sequence labeling problem. In particular, (Stolke et al., 2000; Venkataraman et al., 2003) and (Kim et al., 2010; Chen and Eugenio, 2013; Kumar et al., 2017) have captured dependencies in utterances for dialogue act classification using Hidden Markov Model (HMM) and Conditional Random Field (CRF) respectively. Also, several ways of incorporating such context information in artificial neural networks have been proposed in (Liu, 2017).

The EmotionX shared task consists of detecting emotions for each utterance from EmotionLines dataset. The dataset (Chen et al., 2018) contains dialogues collected from *Friends* TV show scripts and private *Facebook* messenger chats. Each of the utterances has been annotated for one of the eight emotions viz. six basic emotions proposed by (Ekman et al., 1987) and two other emotions viz. *neutral, non-neutral*. The shared task focuses on detecting only four of these eight emotions, namely *joy, sadness, anger* and *neutral*. In this paper, we present our approach to detect emotions in utterances. Inspired by (Kumar et al., 2017), we use Hierarchical Attention Network (HAN) to build context both at utterance and dialogue level. We treat emotion detection at utterance level as a

sequence labeling problem and use a linear chain CRF as a classifier.

2 Proposed Model

The dataset for the task consists of dialogues, each dialogue (D^i) consists of sequence of utterances denoted as $D^i = (u_1, u_2, \ldots u_n)$, where n is the number of utterances in a given dialogue. Each utterance u_j is associated with a target emotion label $y_j \in \mathcal{Y}$. To build context within a dialogue, we consider a moving context window N_k of length k and combine all the utterances within the window with their target labels to create multiple sets of context utterances. These sets of utterances are given as input to our model.

The model consists of HAN (Yang et al., 2016), where the first part is a word-level encoder with the attention layer, encoding each word in an utterance. The second part is an utterance-level encoder, encoding each utterance in the dialogue. The HAN is combined with a linear chain CRF classification layer for detecting emotions. The utterance level emotion detection is treated as a sequence labeling problem based on the fact that the emotion in an utterance depends on emotions of previous utterances. An illustration of complete model comprising of embedding layer, word level encoder, attention layer , utterance level encoder with final layer of CRF classification is depicted in Figure 1.

51

3 Model Desscription

Embedding Layer: A context window N_k consists of k utterances each having l number of words. Each word w_{ij} in an utterance u_j, where $j \in [1,k]$, is embedded to a low-dimensional vector space R^d using an embedding layer (f_{embed}) of size d. It projects the word into representative word vector x_{ij}. We initialize the weights of the embedding layer with pre-trained GloVe embeddings[1].

$$x_{ij} = f_{embed}(w_{ij})$$

Word-level Encoder: We use a bidirectional Gated Recurrent Unit (GRU) (Cho et al., 2014) as the word-level encoder in the hierarchical network to summarize information from both directions for words. The bidirectional GRU contains the forward GRU which reads the utterance u_j from w_{1j} to w_{lj} and a backward GRU which reads from w_{lj} to w_{1j}:

$$\overrightarrow{h}_{ij} = \overrightarrow{GRU}(x_{ij}), i \in [1,l]$$

$$\overleftarrow{h}_{ij} = \overleftarrow{GRU}(x_{ij}), i \in [l,1]$$

The forward hidden state $\overrightarrow{h}_{ij}$ and backward hidden state $\overleftarrow{h}_{ij}$ are concatenated to obtain word encoded representation h_{ij}.

Attention Layer: The intuition for using an attention layer is that a few words in an utterance are more important in identifying an emotion. Moreover, the informativeness of words is context dependent i.e. same set of words contribute differently in different context. We augment the Word-level Encoder with a deep self-attention mechanism (Bahdanau et al., 2014; Baziotis et al., 2017) to obtain a more accurate estimation of the importance of each word. The attention mechanism assigns a weight α_{ij} to each word representation. Formally:

$$r_{ij} = tanh(Wh_{ij} + b)$$

$$\alpha_{ij} = \frac{exp(r_{ij})}{\sum_{i=1}^{l} exp(r_{ij})}$$

$$s_j = \sum \alpha_{ij} h_{ij}$$

---

[1] https://nlp.stanford.edu/projects/glove/

where s_j is the utterance representation.

Utterance-Level Encoder: Similar to Word Level Encoder, the set of utterance representations s_j is passed to a bidirectional GRU to obtain the final representation g_j at utterance level. These representations are passed to CRF classification layer.

Linear Chain CRF: Bidirectional encoder captures dependencies among utterances. To model the dependency among labels, the final utterance representations are passed to the linear chain CRF classifier layer. CRFs are undirected graphical models that predict the optimal label sequence given an observed sequence. For a given context window N_k, the probability of predicting sequence of emotion labels for a set of utterance representations $\overline{g}$ and corresponding emotion label set $\overline{y}$ is

$$P(\overline{y}|\overline{g};w) = \frac{exp(\sum_j w_j F_j(\overline{g},\overline{y}))}{\sum_{y' \in Y} exp(\sum_j w_j F_j(\overline{g},\overline{y'}))}$$

where w_j is the set of parameters corresponding to CRF layer and $F_j(\overline{g},\overline{y})$ is the feature function (Maskey, Spring 2010).

4 Data Preparation

The dataset consists of two sets, viz. 1) dialogues collected from *Friends* TV show script and 2) *Facebook* messenger private chats. Both these datasets have characteristics of *short texts*. We describe our preprocessing strategies for these datasets below.

4.1 Pre-processing

EmotionPush: These are informal chats between two individuals. This data has typical characteristics of short texts. It contains incomplete sentences, informal language, use of emoticons, excessive use of punctuations like '?' and '!'. As a part of preprocessing, we convert all the emoticons to appropriate emotion word. We also replace all occurrences of date and time with named entities **'DATE'** and **'TIME'**. We convert all contracted forms like **'can't'**, **'haven't'** to appropriate expanded forms like **'can not'** and **'have not'**. The dataset contains named entities such as **'PERSON_354'**, **'ORGANIZATION_78'** and

'LOCATION_8'. These entities are important to build the context but they do not appear in word embeddings. We convert all these named entities to pseudo entities which are present in word embeddings but not present in the *EmotionPush* dataset vocabulary.

Accuracy (%)	EmotionPush	Friends
Unweighted	56.73	55.38
neutral	88.2	73.5
anger	21.6	39.8
joy	63.1	57.6
sadness	54	50.6

Table 2: Final results on Test Sets.

Emotion	Precision (%)	Recall (%)	F1 (%)	Accuracy (%)
anger	31	44	36	44
joy	59	64	61	64
neutral	82	85	84	85
sadness	30	61	40	61

Table 3: Experimental results on *EmotionPush* Development Set.

Emotion	Precision (%)	Recall (%)	F1 (%)	Accuracy (%)
anger	36	34	35	34
joy	47	67	55	67
neutral	67	78	72	78
sadness	25	47	33	47

Table 4: Experimental results on *Friends* Development Set.

***Friends - TV Show* scripts**: This dataset contains scene snippets having interaction between two or more speakers. Some of the utterances are incomplete and some have excessive use of punctuations. Unlike *EmotionPush* dataset, there are no emoticons and tagged named entities in this data. We convert the contracted forms as mentioned above and remove extra punctuations. In this dataset, speaker and words uttered by the speaker play an important role in building the context. To incorporate this, we concatenate speaker information to every utterance.

5 Experiments and Results

The EmotionX challenge consists of detecting emotions for each utterance from EmotionLines dataset. Each of the utterances has been annotated for one of the eight emotions, *anger, sadness, joy, fear, disgust, surprise, neutral and non-neutral*. Even though the shared task consists of detection of only four emotions, viz. *joy, sadness, anger* and *neutral*, we consider all emotions in our model. We train the model separately for each dataset. We use pre-trained 100-dimensional GloVe-Tweet embedding for both datasets. These embeddings are used to initialize weights of the embedding layer.

We also consider *word priors* as features. *Word prior* for a *word* is computed as

$$p(w_i|c_j) = \frac{count(w_i, c_j)}{count(c_j)}$$

where $count(w_i, c_j)$ is frequency of *word* w_i in *class* c_j and $count(c_j)$ is total number of words in *class* c_j. We determine *word priors* for every word for all 8 emotion classes and concatenate these 8 features to embedding feature vectors.

The hyper-parameters such as *window length for context window, learning rate, optimizer, early stopping* and *dropout* were tuned for performance during experimentation.

Results on both *EmotionPush* and *Friends* test sets are listed in Table 2. We also report model performance on both the development datasets in Table 3 and Table 4. The model achieved improvement of 22.51% in *Friends* dataset and 36.04% in *EmotionPush* dataset over baseline (Chen et al., 2018) results. We report overall unweighted accuracy of 56.73% on *EmotionPush* test dataset and accuracy of 55.38% on *Friends* test dataset.

6 Discussion

To understand how the context builds over the dialogues, we performed exploratory analysis on both the datasets. In *Friends* dataset, we found some anomalies which can impact the performance of our system.

1. A few dialogues consist of utterances from different scenes which breaks the continuity of the dialogue.

2. Some utterances have scene descriptions as part of the utterance. For example, in record {"speaker": "Joey", **"utterance": "and Phoebe picks up a wooden baseball bat and starts to**

swing as Chandler and Monica enter.)", "emotion": "non-neutral"}, utterance is a scene description and not spoken by any speaker.

3. We also found few utterances having no words but only a punctuation ('.' or '!') which is attached with an emotion. For example,

a) {"speaker": "Rachel", **"utterance"**: **"!"**, "emotion": "non-neutral"}

b) {"speaker": "Phoebe", **"utterance"**: **"."**, "emotion": "non-neutral"}

We did not find such anomalies in *EmotionPush* dataset.

The word embeddings do not have explicit emotion information for words. To incorporate this, we added *word priors* per class to word vectors and examined their effect on the performance of our model. *Word priors* improve the model performance by 17% in *EmotionPush* dataset and 19% in *Friends* dataset. For example, utterances like "Lol weird" and "I also have no shoes lol" belonging to emotion class '*joy*' were misclassified without using word priors as features. Similarly, utterances such as "Sorry he cannot" and "Sorry about that person_107" belonging to emotion class '*sadness*' were also misclassified.

7 Conclusion

In this paper, we present our submission for EmotionX emotion detection challenge. We use Hierarchical Attention Network (HAN) model to learn data representation at both utterance level and dialogue level. Additionally, we formalize the problem as sequence labeling task and use a linear chain Conditional Random Field (CRF) as a classification layer to classify the dialogues in both *Friends* and *EmotionPush* dataset. The model achieved improvement of 22.51% in *Friends* dataset and 36.04% in *EmotionPush* dataset over baseline results. In future, we would like to explore the speaker-listener relation with emotion and lexical features to improve the performance of the system.

References

Dzmitry Bahdanau, Kyunghyun Cho, and Yoshua Bengio. 2014. Neural machine translation by jointly learning to align and translate. *arXiv preprint arXiv:1409.0473*.

Christos Baziotis, Nikos Pelekis, and Christos Doulkeridis. 2017. Datastories at semeval-2017 task 4: Deep lstm with attention for message-level and topic-based sentiment analysis. In *Proceedings of the 11th International Workshop on Semantic Evaluation (SemEval-2017)*, pages 747–754.

Lin Chen and Barbara Di Eugenio. 2013. Multimodality and dialogue act classification in the robohelper project. In *Proceedings of the SIGDIAL*.

Sheng-Yeh Chen, Chao-Chun Hsu, Chuan-Chun Kuo, Ting-Hao (Kenneth) Huang, and Lun-Wei Ku. 2018. Emotionlines: An emotion corpus of multi-party conversations. In *Proceedings of the 11th edition of the Language Resources and Evaluation Conference (LREC 2018)*.

Kyunghyun Cho, Bart Van Merrinboer, Caglar Gulcehre, Dzmitry Bahdanau, Fethi Bougares, Holger Schwenk, and Yoshua Bengio. 2014. Learning phrase representations using rnn encoder-decoder for statistical machine translation. *arXiv preprint arXiv:1406.1078*.

Paul Ekman, Wallace V. Friesen, and Maureen O'Sullivan et al. 1987. Universals and cultural differences in the judgments of facial expressions of emotion. *Journal of Personality and Social Psychology*, 53(4):712–717.

Su Nam Kim, Lawrence Cavedon, and Timothy Baldwin. 2010. Classifying dialogue acts in one-on-one live chats. In *Proceedings of the 2010 Conference on Empirical Methods in Natural Language Processing*.

Uros Krcadinac, Philippe Pasquier, Jelena Jovanovic, and Vladan Devedzic. 2013. Synesketch: An open source library for sentence-based emotion recognition. *IEEE Transactions on Affective Computing*, 4(3):312–325.

Harshit Kumar, Arvind Agarwal, Riddhiman Dasgupta, Sachindra Joshi, and Arun Kumar. 2017. Dialogue act sequence labeling using hierarchical encoder with crf. *arXiv preprint*, arXiv:1709.04250:712–717.

Yang Liu. 2017. Using context information for dialog act classification in dnn framework. In *Proceedings of the 2017 Conference on Empirical Methods in Natural Language Processing*, pages 2170–2178.

Sameer Maskey. Spring 2010. Statistical methods for natural language processing. Course Slides- Week 13 - Language Models, Graphical Models.

Gilad Mishne. 2005. Experiments with mood classification in blog posts. In *Proceedings of ACM SIGIR 2005 Workshop on Stylistic Analysis of Text for Information Access*, pages 321–327.

Saif M Mohammad. 2012a. #emotional tweets. In *Proceedings of the 1st Joint Conference on Lexical and Computational Semantics (*SEM)*, pages 246–255.

Saif M Mohammad. 2012b. From once upon a time to happily ever after: Tracking emotions in mail and books. *Decision Support Systems*, 53(4):730–741.

Daniel Preotiuc-Pietro, H Andrew Schwartz, Gregory Park, Johannes C Eichstaedt, Margaret Kern, Lyle Ungar, and Elizabeth P Shulman. 2016. Modelling valence and arousal in facebook posts. In *Proceedings of Workshop on Computational Approaches to Subjectivity, Sentiment and Social Media Analysis*.

Jacopo Staiano and Marco Guerini. 2014. Depechemood: A lexicon for emotion analysis from crowdannotated news. In *Proceedings of the 52nd Annual Meeting of the Association for Computational Linguistics (ACL)*, pages 427–433.

Andreas Stolke, Klaus Ries, and Noah Coccaro. 2000. Dialogue act modeling for automatic tagging and recognition of conversational speech. *Computation Linguistics*, pages 339–373.

Carlo Strapparava and Rada Mihalcea. 2008. Learning to identify emotions in text. In *Proceedings of the 2008 ACM symposium on Applied Computing*, pages 1556–1560.

Anand Venkataraman, Lucianna Ferrer Andreas Stolcke, and Elizabeth Shriberg. 2003. Training a prosody based dialog act tagger from unlabeled data. In *Proceedings of the 2003 IEEE International Conference on Acoustics, Speech, and Signal Processing*.

Wenbo Wang, Lu Chen, Krishnaprasad Thirunarayan, and Amit P Sheth. 2012. Harnessing twitter big data for automatic emotion identification. In *Proceedings of the 2012 International Conference on Privacy, Security, Risk and Trust (PASSAT) and 2012 International Confernece on Social Computing (SocialCom)*, pages 587–592.

Zichao Yang, Diyi Yang, Chris Dyer, Xiaodong He, Alex Smola, and Eduard Hovy. 2016. Hierarchical attention networks for document classification. In *Proceedings of the 2016 Conference of the North American Chapter of the Association for Computational Linguistics: Human Language Technologies*.

EmotionX-JTML: Detecting emotions with Attention

Johnny Torres
ESPOL University / Guayaquil, Ecuador
`jomatorr@espol.edu.ec`

Abstract

This paper addresses the problem of automatic recognition of emotions in text-only conversational datasets for the EmotionX challenge. Emotion is a human characteristic expressed through several modalities (e.g., auditory, visual, tactile), therefore, trying to detect emotions only from the text becomes a difficult task even for humans. This paper evaluates several neural architectures based on Attention Models, which allow extracting relevant parts of the context within a conversation to identify the emotion associated with each utterance. Empirical results the effectiveness of the attention model for the *EmotionPush* dataset compared to the baseline models, and other cases show better results with simpler models.

1 Introduction

With technology increasingly present in people's lives, human-machine interaction needs to be as natural as possible, including the recognition of emotions. Emotions are an intrinsic characteristic of humans, often associated with mood, temperament, personality, disposition or motivation (Averill, 1980). Moreover, emotions are inherently multimodal, as such, we perceived them in great detail through vision or speech (Jain and Li, 2011).

Detecting emotions from text poses particular difficulties. For instance, an issue that arises from working with conversational text data is that the same utterance (message) can express different emotions depending on its context. The table 1 illustrate the issue with some utterances expressing different emotions with the same word from the challenge datasets (Chen et al., 2018).

Chandler	I guess it must've been some movie I saw. (Neutral)
Chandler	What do you say? (Neutral)
Monica	*Okay! (Joy)*
Chandler	Okay! Come on! Let's go! All right! (Joy)
Rachel	Oh okay, I'll fix that to. What's her e-mail address? (Neutral)
Ross	Rachel! (Anger)
Rachel	All right, I promise. I'll fix this. I swear. I'll-I'll- I'll-I'll talk to her. (Non-neutral)
Ross	*Okay! (Anger)*
Rachel	Okay. (Neutral)

Table 1: Two dialogs from Friends TV scripts. The word "Okay!" denote different emotions depending of the context.

Despite improvements with neural architectures, given an utterance in a conversation without any previous context, it is not always obvious even for human beings to identify the emotion associated. In many cases, the classification of utterances that are too short is hard. For instance, the utterance *'Okay'* can be either an *Agreement* or indicative of *Anger*, for such cases the context plays an essential role at disambiguation. Therefore, using context information from the previous utterances in a conversation flow is a crucial step for improving DA classification.

In this paper, we explore the use of AMs to learn the context representation, as a manner to differentiate the current utterance from its context as well as a mechanism to highlight the most relevant information while ignoring unnecessary parts for emotion classification. We propose and compare different neural-based methods for context representation learning by leveraging a recurrent neu-

Proceedings of the Sixth International Workshop on Natural Language Processing for Social Media , pages 56–60,
Melbourne, Australia, July 20, 2018. ©2018 Association for Computational Linguistics

ral network architecture with LSTM (Hochreiter and Schmidhuber, 1997) or gated recurrent units (GRUs) (Chung et al., 2014) in combination with AMs.

2   Related Work

The identification of emotions is an essential task for understanding natural language and building conversational systems. Previous works on recognizing emotion in text documents consider three categories: keyword-based, learning-based, and hybrid recommendation approaches (Kao et al., 2009).

In recent years, learning methods based on neural architectures have achieved great success. Emotion recognition can be framed as a sentences classification task and has been addressed using various traditional statistical methods, such as Markov Models (HMM) (Stolcke et al., 2000), conditional random fields (CRF) (Zimmermann, 2009) and support vector machines (SVM) (Henderson et al., 2012). Recent work has shown advances in text classification using deep learning techniques, such as convolutional neural networks (CNN) (Kalchbrenner and Blunsom, 2013; Lee and Dernoncourt, 2016), recurrent neural networks (RNNs) (Lee and Dernoncourt, 2016; Ji et al., 2016) and short-term long memory models (LSTM) (Shen and Lee, 2016).

Recent previous works have suggested utilizing context as possible prior knowledge for utterance classification (Lee and Dernoncourt, 2016; Shen and Lee, 2016). Contextual information from preceding utterances has been found to improve the classification performance, but it depends on the specific aspect of the dataset Ortega and Vu (2017). These works highlight that such information should be differentiable from the current utterance information; otherwise, the contextual information could have a negative impact.

Attention mechanisms (AMs) introduced by Bahdanau et al. (2014) have contributed to significant improvements in many natural language processing tasks, for instance machine translation (Bahdanau et al., 2014), sentence classification (Shen and Lee, 2016) and summarization (Rush et al., 2015), uncertainty detection (Adel and Schütze, 2016), speech recognition (Chorowski et al., 2015), sentence pair modeling (Yin et al., 2015), question-answering (Golub and He, 2016), document classification (Yang

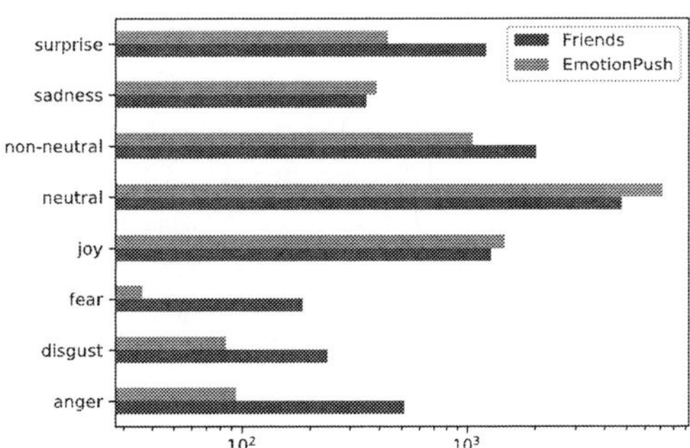

Figure 1: Label distribution of the datasets in the challenge.

et al., 2016) and entailment (Rocktäschel et al., 2015) . AMs let the model decide what parts of the input to pay attention to according to the relevance of the task.

3   Data

Conversational datasets with utterance information are accessible such as movies, television scripts or chat records. Although, despite the importance of emotion detection in conversational systems, most datasets do not have emotion tags, so it is not possible to use such data directly to train models to identify emotions.

The EmotionX challenge provides two annotated datasets with emotions tags. The first, denoted *Friends*, contains the scripts of seasons 1 to 9 of *Friends* TV shows[1]. The second, denoted *EmotionPush*, consist of private conversations between friends on Facebook Messenger collected by the app*EmotionPush* (2016).

Each utterance in the datasets has the same format: the user, the message, and the emotion label. The labels are one of six primary emotions anger, disgust, fear, happiness, sadness, surprise, and neutral defined in (1987). EmotionPush dataset has more skewed label distribution than Friends dataset as shown in Fig.1.

Both Friends and EmotionPush datasets contain 1,000 dialogues. The length distribution of utterances in EmotionPush dataset is much shorter than the length of those of TV show scripts (10.67 vs. 6.84). The EmotionPush dataset is anonymized to hide users' details such as names of real people, locations, organizations, and email addresses. Ad-

---

[1] Scripts of seasons 1-9 of "Friends": `http://www.livesinabox.com/friends/scripts.shtml`

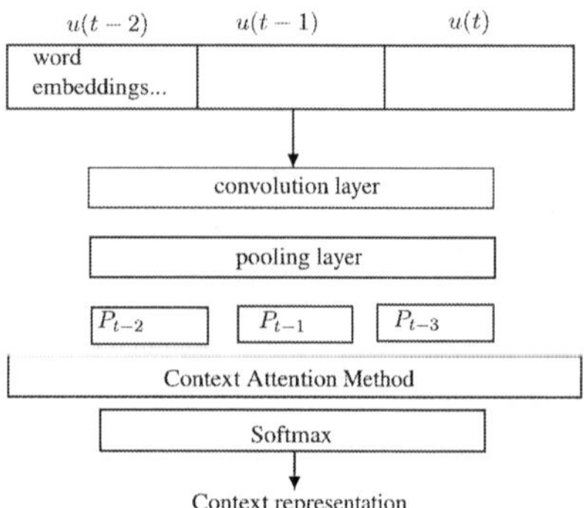

Figure 2: An overview of the architecture of the model based on Attention for classifying emotions in the conversation context.

ditional steps were applied to ensure the privacy of users as described in the dataset paper (Chen et al., 2018).

4   Model

The architecture of the model considers two main parts: the CNN-based utterance representation and the attention mechanism for context representation learning. The Figure 2 shows an overview of the model. The model feeds the context representation into a softmax layer which outputs the posterior of each context utterances given the current utterance.

4.1   Utterance Representation

The proposed architecture uses CNNs for the representation of each utterance. For the emotion classification task, the input matrix represents an utterance and its context (i.e., n previous utterances). Each column of the matrix stores the embeddings of the corresponding word, resulting in d dimensional input matrix $M \in \mathbb{R}^{M \times d}$. The weights of the word embeddings use the 300-dimensional GloVe Embeddings pre-trained on Common Crawl data (Pennington et al., 2014).

The model performs a discrete 1D convolution on an input matrix with a set of different filters of width $|f|$ across all embedding dimensions d, as described by the following equation:

$$(w * f)(x, y) = \sum_{i=1}^{d} \sum_{j=-|f|/2}^{|f|/2} w(i,j) \cdot f(x-i, y-j) \tag{1}$$

After the convolution, the model applies a max pooling operation that stores only the highest activation of each filter. Additionally, the model applies filters with different window sizes 3-5 (multi-windows), which span a different number of input words. Then, the model concatenates all feature maps to one vector which represents the current utterance and its context.

4.2   Attention Layer

The model applies an attention layer to different sequences of input vectors, e.g., representations of consecutive utterances in a conversation. For each of the input vectors $u(t-i)$ at time step $t-i$ in a conversation, the model computes the attention weights for the current time step t as follows:

$$\alpha_i = \frac{exp(f(u(t-i)))}{\sum_{0<j<m} exp(f(u(t-j)))} \tag{2}$$

where f is the scoring function. In the model, f is the linear function of the input $u(t-i)$

$$f(u(t-i)) = W^T u(t-i) \tag{3}$$

where W is a trainable parameter. The output $attentive\_u$ after the attention layer is the weighted sum of the input sequence.

$$attentive\_u = \sum_i \alpha_i u(t-i) \tag{4}$$

4.3   Context Modeling

This paper evaluates different methods to learn the context representation using AMs.

Max   This method applies max-pooling on top of the utterance representations which spans all the contexts and the embedding dimension.

Input   This method applies the attention mechanism directly on the utterance representations. The weighted sum of all the utterances represents context information.

GRU-Attention   This method uses a sequential model with GRU cells on top of the utterance representations to learn the relationship between the context and the current utterance over time. The output of the hidden layer of the last state is the context representation.

		WA	**UWA**	Neu	Joy	Sad	Fea	Ang	Sur	Non
NB	**Friends**	54.9	**57.4**	51.4	57.5	50.0	-	100.0	76.3	36.8
	EmotionPush*	67.3	**57.3**	68.7	76.2	87.5	-	-	100.0	26.7
CNN	**Friends**	59.2	45.2	64.3	60.2	41.2	21.9	46.6	61.5	20.6
	EmotionPush*	71.5	41.7	80.8	46.9	43.7	0.0	27.0	53.8	40.0
CNN-BiLSTM	**Friends**	**63.9**	43.1	74.7	61.8	45.9	12.5	46.6	51.0	8.8
	EmotionPush*	77.4	39.4	87.0	60.3	28.7	0.0	32.4	40.9	26.7
GRU-Attention	**Friends**	57.1	33.4	85.2	46.0	-	3.1	45.1	51.8	30.0
	EmotionPush*	**78.2**	46.8	91.4	65.7	29.9	-	-	58.3	47.1

Table 2: Weighted and unweighted accuracy on Friends and EmotionPush

5 Experiments

For the experiments, neural architectures apply an end-to-end learning approach, i.e., with minimum text preprocessing. For cross-validation, the splitting strategy divides them by the dialogues, similar to (Chen et al., 2018).

The challenge evaluates the performance using the metrics weighted accuracy (WA) and unweighted accuracy (UWA), as defined in equations 5 and 6.

$$WA = \sum_{l \in C} s_l a_l \qquad (5)$$

$$UWA = \frac{1}{|C|} \sum_{l \in C} a_l \qquad (6)$$

where a_l denotes the accuracy of emotion class l and s_l denotes the percentage of utterances in emotion class l.

The Table 2 shows the experimental results including baselines for the emotion detection task. This paper evaluated a Multinomial Naive Bayes (NB) model and the proposed Attention Model (AM). Surprisingly, NB model outperforms neural models for UWA metric in both datasets with 57.4% and 57.3%. This result could be related to the size of the dataset since neural architectures take advantage of learning on large-scale datasets.

The attention model performs well on the EmotionPush dataset but fails to improve on the Friends datasets for WA metric. Further evaluation of the results as depicted in the Fig. 3, show that the label imbalance for *neutral* emotion affects the predictions of other labels.

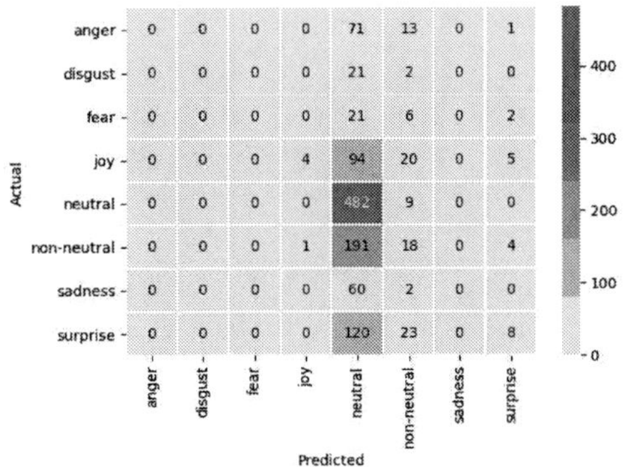

Figure 3: Confusion matrix for the results of Attention Model on the Friend dataset.

6 Conclusions and Future Work

This paper presents a neural attention model for the EmotionX challenge. Attention models take advantage of the context information in conversational datasets for recognizing emotions. The results obtained through several experiments outperformed the baseline methods in some metrics in the emotionPush dataset and was less effective on the Friends dataset.

Despite the promising results with Attention Models, the model struggles to accurately detect ambiguous utterances in the Friend dataset due to the label imbalance and the small scale of it. As such, large-scale conversational corpus with annotated data becomes crucial for pushing the frontiers in emotion recognition.

Attention methods have the potential to provide improved accuracy in detecting emotions in conversational datasets, and future work can explore additional strategies for Attention Models.

References

Heike Adel and Hinrich Schütze. 2016. Exploring different dimensions of attention for uncertainty detection. *arXiv preprint arXiv:1612.06549* .

James R Averill. 1980. A constructivist view of emotion. In *Theories of emotion*, Elsevier, pages 305–339.

Dzmitry Bahdanau, Kyunghyun Cho, and Yoshua Bengio. 2014. Neural machine translation by jointly learning to align and translate. *arXiv preprint arXiv:1409.0473* .

Sheng-Yeh Chen, Chao-Chun Hsu, Chuan-Chun Kuo, Lun-Wei Ku, et al. 2018. Emotionlines: An emotion corpus of multi-party conversations. *arXiv preprint arXiv:1802.08379* .

Jan K Chorowski, Dzmitry Bahdanau, Dmitriy Serdyuk, Kyunghyun Cho, and Yoshua Bengio. 2015. Attention-based models for speech recognition. In *Advances in neural information processing systems*. pages 577–585.

Junyoung Chung, Caglar Gulcehre, KyungHyun Cho, and Yoshua Bengio. 2014. Empirical evaluation of gated recurrent neural networks on sequence modeling. *arXiv preprint arXiv:1412.3555* .

Paul Ekman, Wallace V Friesen, Maureen O'sullivan, Anthony Chan, Irene Diacoyanni-Tarlatzis, Karl Heider, Rainer Krause, William Ayhan LeCompte, Tom Pitcairn, Pio E Ricci-Bitti, et al. 1987. Universals and cultural differences in the judgments of facial expressions of emotion. *Journal of personality and social psychology* 53(4):712.

David Golub and Xiaodong He. 2016. Character-level question answering with attention. *arXiv preprint arXiv:1604.00727* .

Matthew Henderson, Milica Gašić, Blaise Thomson, Pirros Tsiakoulis, Kai Yu, and Steve Young. 2012. Discriminative spoken language understanding using word confusion networks. In *Spoken Language Technology Workshop (SLT), 2012 IEEE*. IEEE, pages 176–181.

Sepp Hochreiter and Jürgen Schmidhuber. 1997. Long short-term memory. *Neural computation* 9(8):1735–1780.

Anil K Jain and Stan Z Li. 2011. *Handbook of face recognition*. Springer.

Yangfeng Ji, Gholamreza Haffari, and Jacob Eisenstein. 2016. A latent variable recurrent neural network for discourse relation language models. *arXiv preprint arXiv:1603.01913* .

Nal Kalchbrenner and Phil Blunsom. 2013. Recurrent convolutional neural networks for discourse compositionality. *arXiv preprint arXiv:1306.3584* .

Edward Chao-Chun Kao, Chun-Chieh Liu, Ting-Hao Yang, Chang-Tai Hsieh, and Von-Wun Soo. 2009. Towards text-based emotion detection a survey and possible improvements. In *Information Management and Engineering, 2009. ICIME'09. International Conference on*. IEEE, pages 70–74.

Ji Young Lee and Franck Dernoncourt. 2016. Sequential short-text classification with recurrent and convolutional neural networks. *arXiv preprint arXiv:1603.03827* .

Daniel Ortega and Ngoc Thang Vu. 2017. Neural-based context representation learning for dialog act classification. *arXiv preprint arXiv:1708.02561* .

Jeffrey Pennington, Richard Socher, and Christopher Manning. 2014. Glove: Global vectors for word representation. In *Proceedings of the 2014 conference on empirical methods in natural language processing (EMNLP)*. pages 1532–1543.

Tim Rocktäschel, Edward Grefenstette, Karl Moritz Hermann, Tomáš Kočiský, and Phil Blunsom. 2015. Reasoning about entailment with neural attention. *arXiv preprint arXiv:1509.06664* .

Alexander M Rush, Sumit Chopra, and Jason Weston. 2015. A neural attention model for abstractive sentence summarization. *arXiv preprint arXiv:1509.00685* .

Sheng-syun Shen and Hung-yi Lee. 2016. Neural attention models for sequence classification: Analysis and application to key term extraction and dialogue act detection. *arXiv preprint arXiv:1604.00077* .

Andreas Stolcke, Klaus Ries, Noah Coccaro, Elizabeth Shriberg, Rebecca Bates, Daniel Jurafsky, Paul Taylor, Rachel Martin, Carol Van Ess-Dykema, and Marie Meteer. 2000. Dialogue act modeling for automatic tagging and recognition of conversational speech. *Computational linguistics* 26(3):339–373.

Shih-Ming Wang, Chun-Hui Li, Yu-Chun Lo, Ting-Hao K Huang, and Lun-Wei Ku. 2016. Sensing emotions in text messages: An application and deployment study of emotionpush. *arXiv preprint arXiv:1610.04758* .

Zichao Yang, Diyi Yang, Chris Dyer, Xiaodong He, Alex Smola, and Eduard Hovy. 2016. Hierarchical attention networks for document classification. In *Proceedings of the 2016 Conference of the North American Chapter of the Association for Computational Linguistics: Human Language Technologies*. pages 1480–1489.

Wenpeng Yin, Hinrich Schütze, Bing Xiang, and Bowen Zhou. 2015. Abcnn: Attention-based convolutional neural network for modeling sentence pairs. *arXiv preprint arXiv:1512.05193* .

Matthias Zimmermann. 2009. Joint segmentation and classification of dialog acts using conditional random fields. In *Tenth Annual Conference of the International Speech Communication Association*.

Towards Automation of Sense-type Identification of Verbs in OntoSenseNet(Telugu)

Sreekavitha Parupalli, Vijjini Anvesh Rao and Radhika Mamidi
Language Technologies Research Center (LTRC)
International Institute of Information Technology, Hyderabad
{sreekavitha.parupalli, vijjinianvesh.rao}@research.iiit.ac.in
radhika.mamidi@iiit.ac.in

Abstract

In this paper, we discuss the enrichment of a manually developed resource of Telugu lexicon, OntoSenseNet. OntoSenseNet is a sense annotated lexicon that marks each verb of Telugu with a primary and a secondary sense. The area of research is relatively recent but has a large scope of development. We provide an introductory work to enrich the OntoSenseNet to promote further research in Telugu. Classifiers are adopted to learn the sense relevant features of the words in the resource and also to automate the tagging of sense-types for verbs. We perform a comparative analysis of different classifiers applied on OntoSenseNet. The results of the experiment prove that automated enrichment of the resource is effective using SVM classifiers and Adaboost ensemble.

1 Introduction

Telugu is morphologically rich and follows different grammatical structures compared to western languages such as English and Spanish. However, to maintain compatibility, the western ideology of rules are adopted in current approaches. Thus, many ideas and significant information of the language is lost. Indian languages are generally fusional (Hindi, English) and agglutinative in nature (Telugu) (Pingali and Varma, 2006). The morphological structure of agglutinative language is unique and capturing its complexity in a machine analyzable and reproducible format is a challenging job (Dhanalakshmi et al., 2009).

OntoSenseNet is a lexical resource developed on the basis of Formal Ontology proposed by (Otra, 2015). The formal ontology follows approaches developed by Yaska, Patanjali and Bhar-

trihari from Indian linguistic traditions for understanding lexical meaning and by extending approaches developed by Leibniz and Brentano in the modern times. This framework proposes that meaning of words are in-formed by intrinsic and extrinsic ontological structures (Rajan, 2015).

Based on this proposed formal ontology, a lexical resource for Telugu language has been developed (Parupalli and Singh, 2018). The resource consists of words tagged with a primary and a secondary sense. The sense-identification in OntoSenseNet for Telugu is done manually by experts in the field. But, further manual annotation of the immense amount of corpus proves to be cost-ineffective and laborious. Hence, we propose a classifier based automated approach to further enrich the resource. The fundamental aim of this paper is to validate and study the possibility of utilizing machine learning algorithms in the task of automated sense-identification.

2 Related Work

The work contributes to building a strong foundation of datasets in Telugu language to enable further research in the field. This section describes previously compiled datasets available for Telugu and past work related to our dataset. We also talk about some recent advancements in NLP tasks on Telugu.

Telugu WordNet, developed as part of IndoWordNet[1], is an exhaustive set of multilingual assets of Indian languages. Telugu WordNet is introduced to capture semantic word relations including but not limited to hypernymy-hyponymy and synonymy-antonymy.

Recent advances are observed in several NLP tasks on Telugu language. (Choudhary et al.,

---

[1] http://www.cfilt.iitb.ac.in/indowordnet/index.jsp

Proceedings of the Sixth International Workshop on Natural Language Processing for Social Media , pages 61–66,
Melbourne, Australia, July 20, 2018. ©2018 Association for Computational Linguistics

2018) developed a siamese network based architecture for sentiment analysis of Telugu and (Singh et al., 2018) utilize a clustering-based approach to handle word variations and morphology in Telugu. But, the ideology that forms the basis of their assumptions lies in western ideology inspired from major western languages. This is due to lack of a large publicly available resource based on the ideology of senses.

3   Data Description

Telugu is a Dravidian language native to India. It stands alongside Hindi, English and Bengali as one of the few languages with official primary language status in India[2]. Telugu language ranks third in the population with number of native speakers in India (74 million, 2001 census)[3]. However, the amount of annotated resources available is considerably low. This deters the novelty of research possible in the language. Additionally, the properties of Telugu are significantly different compared to major languages such as English.

In this paper, we adopt the lexical resource OntoSenseNet for Telugu. The resource consists of 21,000 root words alongside their meanings. The primary and secondary sense of each extracted word is identified manually by the native speakers of language. The paper tries to automate the process and enrich the existing resource. The sense-type classification has been explained below in section 3.2 .

The dataset on which we trained the skip gram model (Mikolov et al., 2013) consists of 27 million words extracted from Telugu Wikipedia dump. Further, we populated our dataset by adding 46,972 sentences from SentiRaama corpus[4] obtained from Language Technologies Research Centre, KCIS, IIIT Hyderabad. Additionally, we added 5410 lines obtained from (Mukku et al., 2016). The corpus that has been assembled is one the of few datasets available in Telugu for research purpose.

---

[2]https://en.wikipedia.org/wiki/Telugu_
language
[3]https://web.archive.org/web/
20131029190612/http://censusindia.gov.
in/Census_Data_2001/Census_Data_Online/
Language/Statement1.htm
[4]https://ltrc.iiit.ac.in/showfile.php?
filename=downloads/sentiraama/

3.1   Morphological Segmentation

Telugu, being agglutinative language, has a high rate of affixes or morphemes per word. Thus, OntoSenseNet resource has little coverage over the Wikipedia data utilized to develop the vector space model. Hence, we applied morphological analysis on both OntoSenseNet and Wikipedia data to segment complex words into its subparts. This leads to an improvement in the coverage of OntoSenseNet resource over the dataset. Thus, the frequency of OntoSenseNet resource increases significantly in the wikipedia corpus. However, the problem of imbalanced class distribution still persists. The addition of this module is empirically justified by the improvements in over-all accuracy metrics shown in the evaluation of results (Section 5).

3.2   Sense-type classification of Verbs

Verbs provide relational and semantic framework for its sentences and are considered as the most important lexical and syntactic category of language. In a single verb many verbal sense-types are present and different verbs share same verbal sense-types. These sense-types are inspired from different schools of Indian philosophies (Rajan, 2013). The seven sense-types of verbs along with their primitive sense along with Telugu examples are given by (Parupalli and Singh, 2018). In this paper, we adopt 8483 verbs of OntoSenseNet as our gold-standard annotated resource. This resource is utilized for learning the sense-identification by classifiers developed in our paper.

- Know—Known - To know.   Examples: *daryptu (investigate), vivarana (explain)*

- Means—End - To do. Examples: *parugettu (run), moyu (carry)*

- Before—After - To move. Examples: *pravha (flow), oragupovu (lean)*

- Grip—Grasp - To have.   Examples: *lgu (grab), vrasatvaga (inherit)*

- Locus—Located - To be. Examples: *dhrapai (depend), kagru (confuse)*

- Part—Whole - To cut.   Examples: *perugu (grow), abhivddhi (develop)*

- Wrap—Wrapped - To bound.   Examples: *dharincaa (wear), raya(shelter)*

4 Methodology & Training

We train a Word2Vec skip-gram model on 2.36 million lines of Telugu text. We train classifiers in one-vs-all setting to get prediction accuracy for each label. Furthermore, we trained and validated on the OntoSenseNet corpus explained in the previous section.

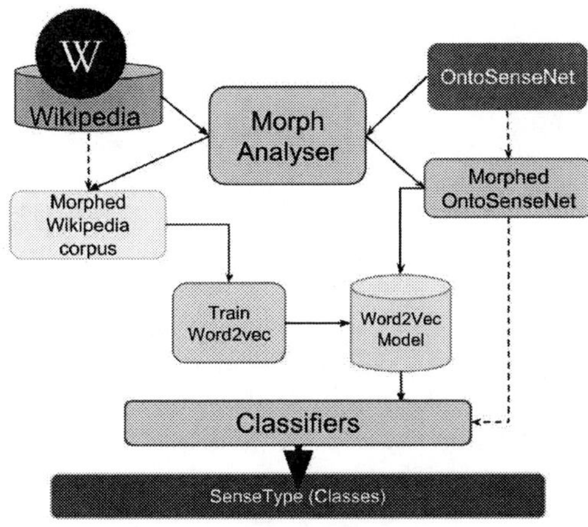

Figure 1: Methodology

4.1 Pre-Processing and Training

Figure 1 depicts the pre-processing steps and overall architecture of our system. To train the vector space embedding (Word2Vec), we initiate by deleting unwanted symbols, punctuation marks, especially ones that do not add significant information. After that, we perform the morphological segmentation of the data and split all the Telugu words in the large Word2Vec training corpus into individual morphemes. For this task, we utilize the Indic NLP library [5] which provides morphological segmentation among other tools, for several Indian languages. Along with splitting morphemes to train Word2Vec, we also stem the words of OntoSenseNet resource. This process of morphological segmentation produces a significant rise in frequencies of morphemes, hence, promoting better vector representations for the Word2Vec model.

Additionally, we only accept embeddings of words present in the OntoSenseNet resource for which an embedding exists in our trained Word2Vec model. This enables us to reduce the problem of resource enrichment to a classification

task. To train the classifiers, we need the word embeddings of the OntoSenseNet's words. However, the words in the resource are also complex and agglutinative in nature. Hence, we stem the OntoSenseNet words too to the smallest root, so that we are able to search them with the Word2Vec embedding model. Finally, the morphed data of embedding training dataset is utilized for training Word2Vec, and stemmed OntoSenseNet words' vectors are extracted to train classifiers described in the next section (Section 3.2). We have used only primary sense-type tagging of the words in OntoSenseNet for enrichment.

4.2 Classifier based Approaches

As each word can have any of the seven sense-types, we have a multi-class classification problem at hand. In Table 1 , we show the multi-class classification accuracies for different classifiers. Additionally, in Figure 2 and Figure 3 we show the one-vs-all accuracies for the seven sense-types of verbs across different classifiers. We then study and analyze these classifier approaches to choose the one with best results. The variants we considered are discussed below:

4.2.1 K Nearest Neighbors

K nearest neighbors is a simple algorithm which stores all available samples and classifies new sample based on a similarity measure (inverse distance functions). A sample is classified by a majority vote of its neighbors, with the sample being assigned to the class most common amongst its K nearest neighbors measured by a distance function.

4.2.2 Support Vector Machines (SVM)

SVM classifier is a supervised learning model that constructs a set of hyperplanes in a high-dimensional space which separates the data into classes. SVM is a non-probabilistic linear classifier. SVM takes the input data and for each input data row it predicts the class to which this input row belongs.

The Gaussian kernel computed with a support vector is an exponentially decaying function in the input feature space, the maximum value of which is attained at the support vector and which decays uniformly in all directions around the support vector, leading to hyper-spherical contours of the kernel function.

`http://anoopkunchukuttan.github.io/ indic_nlp_library/`

4.2.3 Adaboost Ensemble

An AdaBoost classifier is a meta-estimator that begins by fitting a classifier on the original dataset and then fits additional copies of the classifier on the same dataset but where the weights of incorrectly classified instances are adjusted such that subsequent classifiers focus more on difficult cases.

4.2.4 Decision Trees

Decision tree (DT) can be described as a decision support tool that uses a tree like model for the decisions and their likely outcomes. A decision tree is a tree in which each internal (non-leaf) node is labeled with an input feature. Class label is given to each leaf of the tree. But for our work, decision tree gives less accurate results because of over-fitting on the training data. We took the tree depth as 5 for each decision tree.

4.2.5 Random Forest

A Random Forest (RF) classifier is an ensemble of Decision Trees. Random Forests construct several decision trees and take each of their scores into consideration for giving the final output. Decision Trees have a great tendency to overfit on any given data. Thus, they give good results for training data but bad on testing data. Random Forests reduces over-fitting as multiple decision trees are involved. We took the n estimator parameter as 10.

4.2.6 Neural Networks

Multi layer perceptron (MLP) is a feedforward neural network with one or more layers between input and output layer. We call it feedforward as the data flows from input to output layer in a forward manner. Back propagation learning algorithm is used in the training for this sort of network. Multi layer perceptron is found very useful to solve problems which are not linearly separable. The neural network we use for our problem has two hidden layers with the respective sizes being 100 and 25.

5 Evaluation of the Results

We have performed qualitative and quantitative analysis on the results obtained to study the aforementioned experiments.

5.1 Qualitative Analysis

The results (depicted in Figure 2) portray that certain sense-types are predicted with significantly

Classifiers	Before	After
Linear SVM	35.34%	40.72%
Gaussian SVM	36.78%	42.05%
K Nearest Neighbor	26.82%	27.48%
Random Forest	33.76%	37.08%
Decision Trees	33.50%	35.09%
Neural Network	31.67%	40.39%
Adaboost	34.43%	34.68%

Table 1: Improvement of over-all classification accuracy *before* and *after* Morphological Segmentation.

better accuracy than others. The experiments on "To Do" sense-type, especially, result in low accuracy relative to the other sense-types. In the resource, number of samples in one sense-type is higher than others, leaving other sense-types with fewer examples. Furthermore, different types of classifiers produce approximately similar accuracies in identifying particular sense-types. This is due to poor coverage of OntoSenseNet resource in the chosen corpus and also due to difference in distribution of sense-types in the Telugu language. However, we train the classifiers on equal distribution of the sense-types. But, the validation covers the entire OntoSenseNet. Thus, the imbalance in the sense-type distribution of the OntoSenseNet results in low accuracies for the sense-types with more number of samples in the validation set (including "To do").

Additionally, we justify the addition of morphological analyzer due to its added performance boost of over-all accuracy (shown in Table 1).

Furthermore, of the 21,000 root words present in the OntoSenseNet database, only a one-third of the resource have embeddings present in the Word2Vec model, even after stemming. One of the major reasons is that the first volume of the current de facto dictionary was developed in 1936. Language dialects undergo critical evolution with influence from several languages such as Hindi, Tamil and English over time. The corpus adopted in the paper for training the vector space model mainly consists of Telugu Wikipedia data along with some recent collections of various online Telugu News, Books and Poems, that was created relatively recently (in the last decade).

Figure 2 displays that while the relative difference among classifiers is less as compared to performance across sense types, there are still some

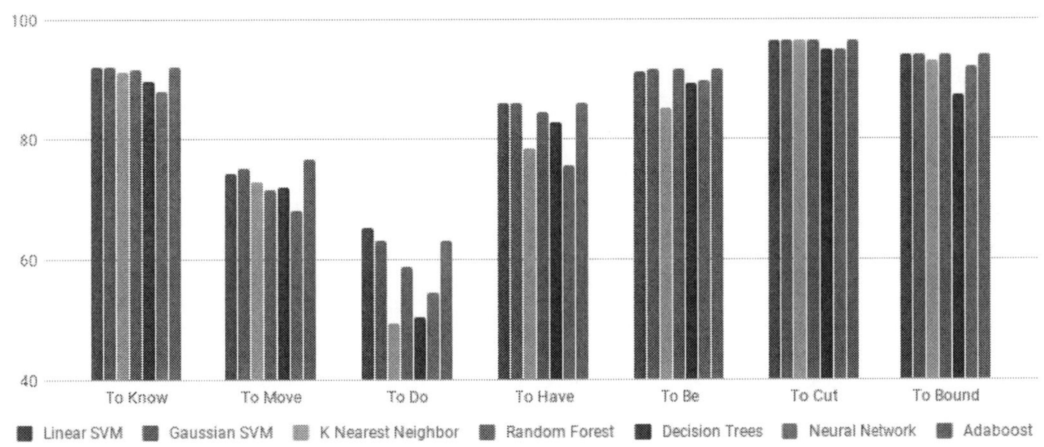

Figure 2: Accuracies for all the sense-types of verbs when the classifiers are trained in one-vs.-all setting.

performance patterns that are observed. Across majority of the metrics, Gaussian SVM performs the best and outperforms all the classifiers including linear SVM indicating that the data is linearly separable in higher dimensions. Another commonly noted observation is that of Decision Tree versus Random Forest. Decision Trees tend to perform worse than Random Forest as they overfit on large data. However, Random Forests circumvent this problem by having multiple or an ensemble of decision trees, leading to a better performance, which is also reflected in our experiments.

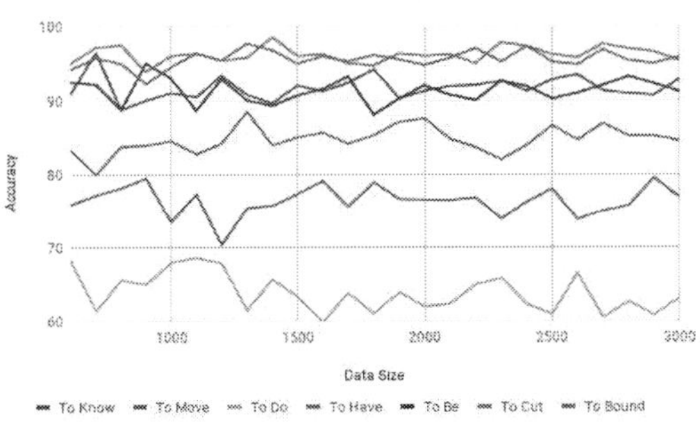

Figure 3: Accuracy of each sense-type across changing number of data samples using a Gaussian SVM.

5.2 Quantitative

For quantitative analysis, to understand the correlation between accuracy performance and training size, we choose Gaussian SVM as the classifier because it gives the best results (Figure 2). The graph of accuracy of each sense-type, given the classifier is a Gaussian SVM, is illustrated in Figure 3. A major observation from the results is the consequence of class imbalance. The initial increase in data results in a boost in performance of the model. But, as the number of samples in the test data increases, the class imbalance of the validation dataset becomes more prominent leading to fluctuations in the accuracy.

6 Conclusion and Future Work

Automatic enrichment of OntoSenseNet is attempted in this work. We compare several classifiers and test, validate their effectiveness in the task. Qualitative analysis of the classifiers empirically proves that Gaussian SVM is the best for the task of enriching OntoSenseNet. Quantitative analysis proves that, given a method to handle class imbalance, the model's effectiveness is directly proportional to the amount of training data. A continuation to this paper could be handling adjectives and adverbs available in OntoSenseNet for Telugu. Additionally, we identify a case of clustering-based extension like fuzzy k means where each word has a probability of belonging to each sense-type, rather than completely belonging to just one. This helps in identification of the secondary senses of verbs in OntoSenseNet.

6.1 Acknowledgments

We would like to thank Nurendra Choudary for helping us in formulation and development of this idea.

References

Nurendra Choudhary, Rajat Singh, Ishita Bindlish, and Manish Shrivastava. 2018. Emotions are universal: Learning sentiment based representations of resource-poor languages using siamese networks. *arXiv preprint arXiv:1804.00805*.

V Dhanalakshmi, RU Rekha, Arun Kumar, KP Soman, S Rajendran, et al. 2009. Morphological analyzer for agglutinative languages using machine learning approaches. In *Advances in Recent Technologies in Communication and Computing, 2009. ARTCom'09. International Conference on*, pages 433–435. IEEE.

Tomas Mikolov, Ilya Sutskever, Kai Chen, Greg S Corrado, and Jeff Dean. 2013. Distributed representations of words and phrases and their compositionality. In *Advances in neural information processing systems*, pages 3111–3119.

Sandeep Sricharan Mukku, Nurendra Choudhary, and Radhika Mamidi. 2016. Enhanced sentiment classification of telugu text using ml techniques. In *SAAIP@ IJCAI*, pages 29–34.

Spandana Otra. 2015. *TOWARDS BUILDING A LEXICAL ONTOLOGY RESOURCE BASED ON INTRINSIC SENSES OF WORDS*. Ph.D. thesis, International Institute of Information Technology Hyderabad.

S. Parupalli and N. Singh. 2018. Enrichment of OntoSenseNet: Adding a sense-annotated Telugu lexicon. *ArXiv e-prints*.

Prasad Pingali and Vasudeva Varma. 2006. Hindi and telugu to english cross language information retrieval at clef 2006. In *CLEF (Working Notes)*.

Kavitha Rajan. 2013. Understanding verbs based on overlapping verbs senses. In *51st Annual Meeting of the Association for Computational Linguistics Proceedings of the Student Research Workshop*, pages 59–66.

Kavitha Rajan. 2015. Ontological classification of verbs based on overlapping verb senses.

Rajat Singh, Nurendra Choudhary, and Manish Shrivastava. 2018. Automatic normalization of word variations in code-mixed social media text. *arXiv preprint arXiv:1804.00804*.

Improving Classification of Twitter Behavior During Hurricane Events

Kevin Stowe, Jennings Anderson, Martha Palmer, Leysia Palen, Ken Anderson
University of Colorado, Boulder, CO 80309
`[kest1439, jennings.anderson, mpalmer, palen, kena]@colorado.edu`

Abstract

A large amount of social media data is generated during natural disasters, and identifying the relevant portions of this data is critical for researchers attempting to understand human behavior, the effects of information sources, and preparatory actions undertaken during these events. In order to classify human behavior during hazard events, we employ machine learning for two tasks: identifying hurricane related tweets and classifying user evacuation behavior during hurricanes. We show that feature-based and deep learning methods provide different benefits for tweet classification, and ensemble-based methods using linguistic, temporal, and geospatial features can effectively classify user behavior.

1 Introduction

Identifying relevant information for natural disaster and other hazards is a difficult task, particularly in social media, which is often noisy. Understanding people's behavior during events is an important task for both researchers studying human responses to hazards after events and real-time processing of disaster-related information. Keyword searches can be an effective first pass, but are insufficient to fully understand user behavior and can generate large numbers of both false positives and false negatives. To improve our ability to study behavior during crisis events, we employ supervised machine learning for two tasks: identifying tweets that are relevant to hurricane events and classifying Twitter users' evacuation behavior.

2 Task One: Improving Tweet Classification

Twitter data is often difficult to understand due to limited length of tweets and the noise inherent in the medium. As a result, there is a variety of research in attempting to effectively identify and classify tweets. There are multiple studies in classification of flu-related tweets (Culotta, 2010; Aramaki et al., 2011). One relevance classification approach is Lamb et al. (2013), which initially classifies tweets for relevance and then applies finer-grained classifiers. They build classifiers using syntactic and Twitter-specific features to detect awareness versus infection, self versus others, and whether tweets are relevant to the flu or not.

Sriram et al. (2010) propose a somewhat more specific system, classifying tweets into general categories like news, events, and opinions, achieving accuracies between .85 and .95 depending on category. Sankaranarayanan et al. (2009) perform a similar task, classifying tweets into either news or non-news. Recently, the work of Volkova et al. (2017) attempts to classify suspicious and trusted tweets. They find that deep learning models outperform feature-based models, but linguistics features can be helpful. They report F1 scores of between .88 and .92 depending on the category classified.

For our first task of relevant tweet classification, we employ supervised machine learning to predict whether individual tweets are relevant to a hurricane. This study focuses on the Hurricane Sandy event in October of 2012. This hurricane made landfall on the eastern seaboard of the United States on October 29, causing massive damage to many areas including New York and New Jersey. To collect data for this event, we initially performed a collection capturing all tweets

Proceedings of the Sixth International Workshop on Natural Language Processing for Social Media, pages 67–75,
Melbourne, Australia, July 20, 2018. ©2018 Association for Computational Linguistics

Tweet	Relevant
For the love of that money.....	n
Lol the struggle for gas and Power 💡📱🔋	y
where u been hiding at through this storm	y
Smh I still don't get to play Halo 4 yet...	n

Table 1: Sample Tweet Classification Stream

Model	F1	Prec	Recall
Stowe et al (SVM Baseline)	.769	.886	.678
Multi-layer Perceptron	**.834**	.886	.788
Convolutional NN	.815	.874	.763

Table 2: Tweet Classification Results

using the following keywords:

DSNY, cleanup, debris, frankenstorm, garbage, hurricane, hurricanesandy, lbi, occupysandy, perfectstorm, sandy, sandycam, stormporn, superstorm

This generated approximately 22.2 million unique tweets from 8 million users. We then identified users who had geo-tagged tweets within areas that were heavily impacted by the event. This allowed us capture users who were likely to be significantly impacted and local to the event. From these we randomly selected 105 users, collecting the tweets from a week before landfall to a week after, resulting in 25,474 tweets. We annotated these tweets for hurricane relevance (two annotators, agreement approximately .9). Our task is to classify for each user which tweets are relevant (Table 1).

We developed a standard feature-based machine learning classifier and compare it to several deep learning approaches. We split our data into training (60%), validation (20%), and test (20%) sets, tuning each model on the validation set and evaluating on the test data.

2.1 Feature-based

As a baseline for feature-based classification, we follow the setup and features of Stowe et al. (2016), who employ support vector machines and linguistic features to classify hurricane related tweets. As a baseline, we re-implement this approach, leaving out features that appeared to have negligible contribution. We used the following features from their set:

- Bag of words based on Pointwise Mutual Information (PMI) for unigrams, bigrams, and trigrams. We chose the n terms with highest PMI for positive and negative classes, with n set to 200 as was determined in validation. Selecting the bag of words lexicon based on PMI significantly improves results over using the full set of words.

- The time of the target tweet, using a one-hot vector representing the time bin of the target tweet. Through validation we chose to use 384 bins, or one per hour.

- Average word embeddings for each tweet. We experimented with using Google News vectors generated using word2vec (Mikolov et al., 2013) and Glove Twitter embeddings (Pennington et al., 2014). We selected the Google News vectors, as they had the best performance.

For comparison, we employ two deep learning approaches: a multi-layered perceptron (MLP) and a convolutional neural network (CNN).

2.2 Multi-layered Perceptron (MLP)

For our MLP, we started with inputing each tweet as a collection of words, padded up to length 25. We used an embedding layer of dimension 300 using the pretrained Google News vectors, and fed this through a 50 node dense layer using a rectified linear unit (relu) activation with a dropout rate of .5. This was then fed into the output layer, using sigmoid activation to predict either relevant or irrelevant. The model was trained using categorical hinge loss, running 50 epochs.

2.3 Convolutional Neural Network (CNN)

Convolutional neural networks incorporate local word context using convolutions of words within a contextual window, and have proven effective in a variety of sentence classification tasks (Kim, 2014; Li et al., 2017). As tweets can be considered a sentence, we experiment with using CNNs for relevance classification.

We follow the approach of Kim (2014), using an embedding layer (from the Google News vectors), which is then fed into a convolutional layer. We use kernel sizes of 2, 3, and 4, with 16 filters per kernel size. We use max pooling to combine the outputs, with a pool size of 4. Finally, we use a fully connected layer to the binary output nodes, using sigmoid activation to predict relevance.

Both deep learning models improve over the re-implemented SVM baseline. However, the CNN doesn't improve over the basic multi-layer perceptron.

2.4 Effects of Context

Sentence classification is a common task, and it has been applied effectively to tweets. However, most classification for Twitter data is done on individual tweets, without regard to their larger context. This causes an impoverished information environment: knowing the context a tweet is present in from a user's perspective provides valuable information about the meaning of the tweet.

Because of this, we experimented with using contextual models to predict tweet relevance. We experimented with using the same SVM model above, experimenting with expanding the feature window to include more context, as well as adding additional contextual tweets the MLP model. In both cases, we used contextual windows from 1-16 words before and after the tweets. We found that performance decreased consistently as more context was added, and using only the target tweet yielded the best results

We also experimented with using sequence taggers, specifically a long short-term memory (LSTM) network. We input each user as a training batch, treating the tweets they produced chronologically as a sequence. Our results using the LSTM model were much lower than the non-sequence taggers (.65 compared to .83). Tuning model size and dropout, as well as adding bidirectional and attention layers failed to significantly improve performance.

From the data, it appears that context is vital for determining tweet relevance, but our models have not been able to capture the significance. We believe this is due to the irregular nature of helpful context. In tweet streams, it is often the case that one particular tweet in the context is necessary to understand the target, but the location in context of the tweet is not consistent. Because of this inconsistency, the model cannot reliable determine which element in context is contributing the necessary information. As a future goal, we aim to incorporate better methods of representing context that can filter out contextual tweets that likely don't influence the target.

2.5 Effects of Data Size

As each event is unique and other kinds of natural hazards are likely to pose completely new problems, we would ideally like to be able to generate new classifiers with as little data as possible. We experiment with varying the size of our training data to assess how much is necessary to reach peak performance. We held out 20% of our data as a test set, and then trained classifiers incrementally, adding 100 instances of training data at a time. We also tested the effectiveness of combining models by implementing a combined classifier. This classifier uses the output of the MLP and the SVM as features for training a logistic regression classifier. The results of these classifiers as training data is added are shown in Figure 1.

The SVM achieves strong recall very quickly, at over .8 with only 5,000 training instances. The perceptron follows an opposite pattern, with precision over .9 at 5,000 but very low recall. The SVM is consistently improving at around 2,500 training instances, and shows only minimal improvement after 7,5000. The perceptron is much more irregular, being ineffective until nearly 7,500 instances and leveling off near 12,500.

We believe that precision is more important for this task, as there are such a large number of tweets available, it is more important to identify tweets correctly than to capture all of them. However, the perceptron takes more data to be consistent. Combining classifiers in this case doesn't improve performance over either the SVM or MLP individually, although the logistic regression approach is comparable. The best approach for extending classification novel events is to assess whether precision or recall is more important, and select the individual classifier that fits the goals of the research.

Classification of tweets can be improved by employing deep learning models, which significantly outperforms feature-based methods. Comparisons to other work are difficult to the differences in tasks. We do not achieve the F1 scores of Volkova et al. (2017) or Sriram et al. (2010), both between .85 and .95, but the tasks are likely too different for meaningful comparison.

3 Task 2: Evacuation Classification

Tweet classification provides information about user behavior as users tweet about their experiences and actions as the events are unfolding. At a broader level, we can also use tweet streams from a user to attempt to determine their evacuation behavior during an event. For this, we need to examine their entire stream and understand both their

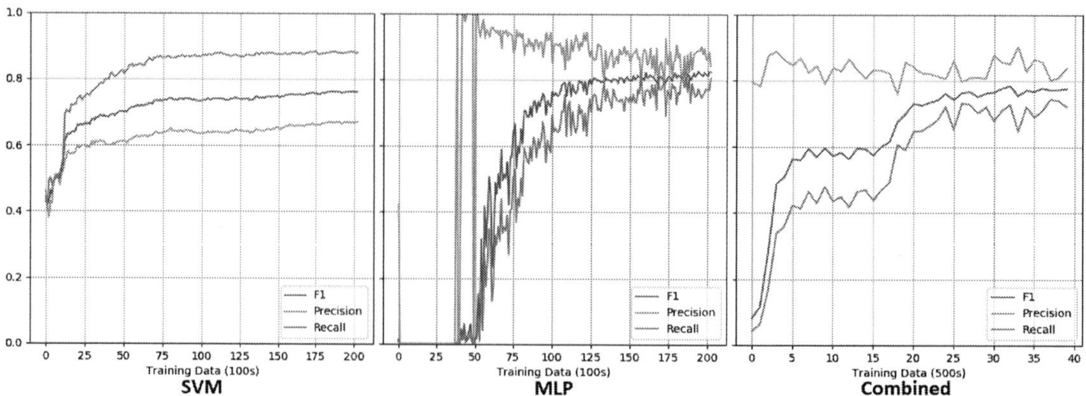

Figure 1: Classification as Training Data is Added

language and their actions. In this section we describe our annotation of Twitter users' evacuation behavior, and show that linguistic and geospatial data can used for classification.

User level classification for Twitter users is a well known problem for many domains. One common task is identifying political affiliation. Both linguistic and non-linguistic features have proven effective in classifying political leanings of users in Twitter data (Tatman et al., 2017). Preoiuc-Pietro et al. (2017) provide a method for identifying whether users are liberal or conservative, and point to a variety of user level classifications that can be predictive of political ideology. These user-level attributes apply generally; we intend to classify users based on a particular behavior they engage in (evacuation or sheltering in place).

More similar is Sanagavarapu et al. (2017), who predict whether users participate in events that they are tweeting about. They use linguistics features coupled with support vector machines to predict users' participation in specific events, which parallels our task of predicting a user's event-related behavior.

In the domain of crisis informatics, recent work by Martín et al. (2017) identifies evacuation patterns, using aggregates of geo-located tweets as well as particular user behaviors. However, they don't empirically validate their observations, and thus don't attempt statistic learning for classification. Another study from Yang et al. (2017) studies user behavior during crisis events, using linguistic and spatial features to analyze shifting sentiment during Hurricane Sandy. While they focus on keyword tweets clustered geographically, they show that geospatial features are helpful for anal-

ysis of user attitudes during crises.

3.1 Data

Our analysis is focused on users that are potentially at risk, but these users are difficult to identify due to the noisiness of Twitter data. To alleviate this problem, we attempt to identify vulnerable users using geospatial information. For our data, location-enabled tweets include any tweet returned by the Twitter API with a precise point-location attribute. This is sometimes the precise latitude and longitude of the user's mobile device; however, and more common in recent years, these are more general locations that, while encoded in the tweet as a single geographic coordinate, represent businesses or more general regional locations. These often include cross-posts from other social media services that track location such as FourSquare, Swarm, or Instagram. Examples of these locations include: "Starbucks" (as an exact store) or "South Beach" (as a region).

For Hurricane Sandy, we used bounding boxes for Evacuation Zone A in New York City as well as boundaries of the coastal counties of New Jersey to define geographically vulnerable areas. Each of these areas were under mandatory evacuation orders and generally exhibited high levels of geographic risk to the storm.

3.2 Spatial Clustering

To reduce the noise and identify the most important locations for a user, we apply a clustering algorithm to all of the tweets for a given user. We use Density Based Spatial Clustering (DBScan) to cluster each user's tweets based on their coordinates (Ester et al., 1996). We chose this algorithm

70

for two reasons. First, it does not require that
we declare a particular number of clusters ahead
of time. Since we cannot make any assumptions
about a user's consistent located-enabled Twitter
activity, we do not know how many clusters will
best represent the recurring locations for any given
user. Second, it does not require that all points be
classified. This allows for rigid, similar sized clusters with separate unclassifiable points. Through
empirical analysis of our data, this is critical to understanding a user's recurring tweet locations because users tend to tweet very irregularly (spatially
speaking): on a moving bus or train, for example.

Once these spatially outlying points are marked
as noise, we focus analysis on locations of consistent, recurring Twitter behavior, such as one's residence or workplace. Our clustering parameters
require a user to have at least five tweets within
100 meters of one-another within the three-month
period of study. These parameters are stricter than
those used in Jurdak et al. (2015) and were decided
through empirical analysis of spatial tweet distributions of a few users. Since the purpose of the
clusters is to identify areas of work or residence
that may be at risk of a coastal hazard, 100 meters
allows the clustering to account for some noise and
inaccuracies in the reported location over the entire study period. We remove any users who do not
have at least one identifiable cluster.

3.3 Temporal Clustering

To learn about a user's regular (non-storm) Twitter behavior, we identify their temporal tweeting
patterns up to the time of the storm. To general-
ize this over the entire period of study, we look
specifically at times of tweets per week. Given the
regular diurnal Twitter activity among users, we
next cluster the tweets by time of day and day of
week to establish a weekly tweeting distribution
for each user. Krumm et al. (2013) use a similar
method of discerning home locations based on the
time one is active, based on the American Time
Use Survey. First, we distinguish days as weekdays or weekends and then split these days into
six four-hour periods. The resulting 12 time bins
distinguish between common home and working
hours. Of these times, weekday evenings generally see the most Twitter activity.

3.4 Spatio-Temporal Clustering: Home Locations

Co-occurrences between the geo- and temporal-
clusters identify likely home clusters as distinct
from work or school clusters. For example, if
a user's tweets from *geo-cluster A* occur primarily during weekdays from 12-4pm while *geo-
cluster B* primarily includes tweets from weekday evenings from 8pm-12am, then we may in-
fer that *geo-cluster A* could represent that user's
school or workplace while *cluster B* could represent their home. To perform this identification of a
user's before-storm home location, we then identify geo-clusters that commonly co-occur with the
following specific time bins that represent *home
times*: Weekdays between 12-4am, 4-8am, and
8pm-12am. The geometric centroid of the cluster with the most tweets during these times is said
to be the user's home location.

Note that these home locations don't necessar-
ily represent where the user lives. While we qual-
itatively observe that these home locations usually appear to be correct, they also can be gyms,
offices, and other places that the user typically
tweets from. We'll see in section 3.6 that home
location information is a good predictor of evacuation behavior, regardless of whether it represents
an actual 'home' or merely a location of consistent behavior for a particular user when daily life
is not interrupted by a major storm. If this location
lands within the geographically vulnerable areas
under mandatory evacuation described above, this
user is said to geographically vulnerable. Furthermore, the empirically observed accuracy of this
approach to determining a user's home location invites further research that optimizes the clustering
(both spatially and the temporal bins) to improve
detection of a user's home-location based on their
geo-located social media activity.

The simplicity of our approach combined with
the observed accuracy suggests that users are
likely not aware of the extent and accuracy of the
public geo-trace they are producing through their
social media activity. All of the tweets used for
this work were posted to the user's Twitter timeline for public consumption. As a first step to pro-
tecting user's privacy, we do not publish the user's
Twitter handle, against the formal guidelines for
republication of Twitter data. Further, we inten-
tionally do not show a larger-scale rendering of
their calculated home location. For these reasons,

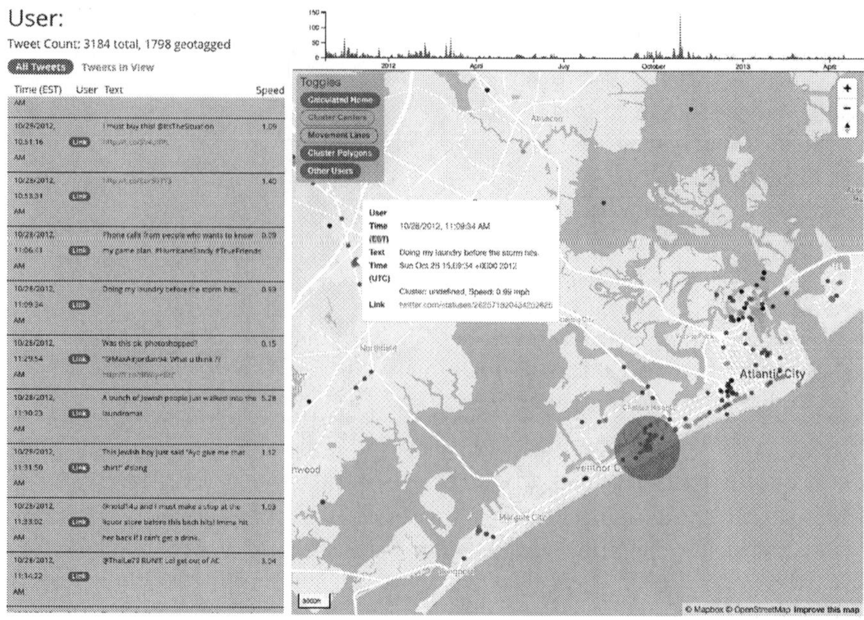

Figure 2: A screen shot of our annotation tool. The timeline across the top shows this user was most active at time of landfall. Tweets are displayed in chronological order on the left and an interactive map on the right shows tweets, colored by different clusters. The transparent blue circle indicates the calculated home location. Just before landfall and throughout the duration of the storm, the user is tweeting from a different location (see popup) further inland than their calculated home: a strong signal of evacuation.

and in part because the data is now over five years old, we choose to publish the data as-is, without their identifiable Twitter handle. These are self-imposed ethical responsibilities because as far as the data providers are concerned, this is public data. We hope this situation invites further conversation around social media privacy, information sharing, and more formalized ethical standards in social media research concerning these highly personalized data traces.

3.5 Annotation

Our perception of spatially derived evacuation patterns is clear: geographically vulnerable users tweet from their vulnerable locations before the storm and then do not tweet from this location at landfall. However, few users have such clear cut movement profiles. Furthermore, programmatically searching for this behavior yields a troubling amount of false positives. Just because a user is not tweeting from home does not mean they have chosen to evacuate. These complex user behaviors led us to develop a tool and annotation process for determining individuals responses to the events.

Our annotation involves determining if a user evacuated, sheltered in place, or their behavior was unclear based on the available data. Each user was given one of these categories based on both their tweet content and movement patterns as inferred by manual inspection. This involved developing a framework for displaying tweets on a map over a sliding window of time, allowing annotators to easily identify what users were saying at which locations, thus giving the capability to determine possible evacuation behavior quickly and accurately. Using this tool, we tagged 200 users with evacuation, sheltering in place, or unclear, along with a confidence score for evacuation and sheltering in place.

Note that this annotation process has inherent problems: we can only indicate whether we believe a user evacuated based on their tweets and geo-location. We can not prove that any user evacuated based only on these limited resources. So while annotators tend to agree on whether they believe a person took a particular action (κ=.705 for tweets annotators were confident of the correct answer), the analysis is not objectively verified.

Tweets	Coords	Time
Hurricane Party!	40.6,-73.9	12/29 14:03
I had to evacuate this is bull	40.8,-72.9	12/29 19:26
East NY 4ever!	40.8,-73.4	12/30 11:45
Prediction	Evacuated	

Table 3: Sample Evacuation Prediction

3.6 Classification

We employ supervised machine learning to predict each user's possible actions during each event. This is done by employing word embeddings to represent tweet semantics combined with temporal and spatial features generated from tweet metadata. We treat each user's full contextual stream (all the tweets they produced from a week before to a week after landfall) as a document (see Table 3 for an example). As a baseline for classification, we start with the average embedding over all the words in the contextual stream, providing a simple document-level embedding.

3.6.1 Temporal Information

We've seen from section 3.1 that users' tweeting behavior varies greatly based on time. In order to capture this, we split each user into a series of time bins. For each bin, we generate the average embedding over all the tweets in the time slice. These embeddings are concatenated and supplied as input to the classifier. We experimented with a variety of bin sizes from 4 hours to 4 days. Smaller bins capture more specific data, but are often contain too few tweets to be useful. Larger bins provide more consistent, general information.

3.6.2 Spatial Information

We combine information from geo-tags with word embeddings to generate more accurate representations of user behavior. For each temporal bin generated above, we calculate a handful of spatial features. First, we calculate the average location of the user during that bin, using the mean latitude and longitude of each tweet in that bin that contains a geo-tag. We then use this to determine the geometric distance from the average location in that bin to the calculated home location from section 3.4. This is a simple scalar feature indicating their distance from their typical home location. As a second spatial feature, we calculated the average distance of each tweet within a bin from the starting location of that bin, which indicates the average amount the user moved during that time.

3.6.3 Relevance Filtering

In most cases the majority of tweets a user produces are irrelevant to a particular event. This creates additional noise in each time bin, making it hard to predict behavior. We employ the relevance classifier above, trained on the full dataset, and use it to predict relevance for each user's tweets. We then restrict the features above to only tweets that the classifier deemed relevant.

We evaluate Logistic Regression, Support Vector Machines, and Naive Bayes algorithms for user classification. We experimented with deep learning methods, but they showed much lower results, perhaps due to the small size of the dataset. Support vector machines provided the best performance on the baseline, and was used to evaluate additional features. We performed 10-fold cross validation over users. Table 4 shows the results of adding each feature type and bin size. Each column represents the size of the temporal bin used. The "All" column uses only one bin, with all the user's tweets averaged. In this case the Distance from Home Location is the distance from their overall average location to the location of their calculated home location from section 3.4.

Bin sizes from 1 to 4 days are most effective, with distance from home location being the best feature. Note that we did not objectively verify these home locations: the classifier uses this feature effectively regardless of whether it represents the user's real home, or just a location they regularly tweet from. Relevance filtering does not provide consistent improvement, which may be due to data sparsity. Any filtering reduces the amount of tweets available for each bin, making the classification task more difficult.

These four features (word embeddings, temporal and spatial information, and relevance filtering) all provide different ways of understanding user behavior. Because they represent the data in different ways, they are capable of classifying different sections of the data accurately. We leverage this by employing ensemble classification employing these features.

3.6.4 Ensemble Classification

To combine feature's benefits, we use each of the 48 classifiers generated for Table 4. We combine these classifiers incrementally, starting with the classifiers that had the best performance in cross validation. We trained each classifier on 50% of the data and evaluated it on the remaining 50%.

Feature	4 hours	8 hours	1 day	2 days	4 days	All Days
Word Embedding Average	.467	.491	.529	.505	.555	*.529*
+Relevance Filter	.481	.484	.489	**.606**	.526	.533
Distance from Home Location	.610	.692	**.695**	.686	.639	.674
+Relevance Filter	.657	.621	.672	.661	.608	.664
Average Movement per Time Bin	.484	.506	.504	.587	**.641**	.533
+Relevance Filter	.541	.501	.526	.566	.574	.508
All	.533	.504	**.550**	.524	**.550**	.531
+Relevance Filter	.484	.485	.493	.486	.534	.534

Table 4: Classification Results (F1) for Each Feature Type and Bin Size. **Bold** indicates the best result for that feature, *italics* is our word embedding baseline.

We then weighted each classifier's classification by the F1 score it received in cross validation on the training set. This allowed for more classifiers to be added providing additional information, but still favoring the classifiers that performed best in training. Results of the incremental addition of classifiers are shown in Figure 3.

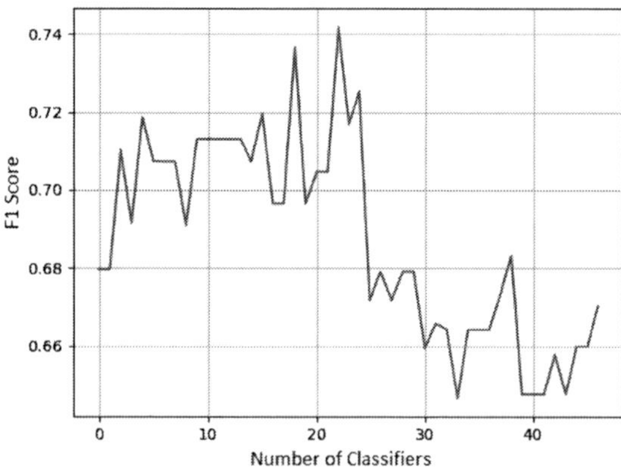

Figure 3: System performance (F1) as classifiers are added.

3.7 Analysis

Adding additional classifiers improves performance initially but after a certain point the added classifiers decrease performance. The best performance is achieved using around 20 classifiers, which include those trained on all three individual features for a wide variety of time bins. While the first 16 classifiers are based on distance from home cluster, the addition of word embedding- and movement-based classifiers can yield improved performance. As more classifiers are added, performance drops, likely because when the less accurate classifiers are added they degrade performance.

Performance on user classification varies greatly depending on the classification method and windows used. The basic word embedding baseline over all tweets performs poorly (.529). Prediction based on distance from a user's home location using a bin size of 1 day is the best single classifier (.695), and distance from their calculated home performs best across all bin sizes. The best F1 achieved through ensemble methods is .741, a considerable improvement over the performance of the best individual classifier .694.

While it is difficult to compare these results to previous work, as the task has not yet been attempted, there are some relevant comparisons. Sanagavarapu et al. (2017) report classifying users' participation in events with F1 scores varying from .52 to .74. They show that different features yield different results based on the time period, which parallels our results.

4 Conclusions

Evacuation behavior is difficult to predict, but can be done by leveraging both linguistic and geospatial features. More data and better representations of movement could improve this classification, but the changing nature of Twitter use is making precise geospatial data increasingly rare and harder to make us of for behavior classification in this medium.

Our relevance classifier achieves an F1 score of near .83, and needs refinement to be effectively employed in this domain. Further improvements to classification can be made be effectively incorporating tweet context. In order to make use of this classification, we intend to experiment with real-time relevance classification, which will allow us to better understand user behavior live as events unfold.

References

Eiji Aramaki, Sachiko Maskawa, and Mizuki Morita. 2011. Twitter catches the flu: Detecting influenza epidemics using Twitter. In *Conference on Empirical Methods in Natural Language Processing (EMNLP)*, pages 1568–1576.

Aron Culotta. 2010. Towards detecting influenza epidemics by analyzing twitter messages. In *Proceedings of the First Workshop on Social Media Analytics*, SOMA '10, pages 115–122, New York, NY, USA. ACM.

Martin Ester, Hans-Peter Kriegel, Jörg Sander, and Xiaowei Xu. 1996. A Density-Based Algorithm for Discovering Clusters in Large Spatial Databases with Noise. *2nd International Conference on Knowledge Discovery and Data Mining*, pages 226–231.

Raja Jurdak, Kun Zhao, Jiajun Liu, Maurice Abou-Jaoude, Mark Cameron, and David Newth. 2015. Understanding human mobility from Twitter. *PLoS ONE*, 10(7):e0131469.

Yoon Kim. 2014. Convolutional neural networks for sentence classification. In *Proceedings of the 2014 Conference on Empirical Methods in Natural Language Processing (EMNLP)*, pages 1746–1751, Doha, Qatar. Association for Computational Linguistics.

John Krumm, Rich Caruana, and Scott Counts. 2013. Learning likely locations. In *Lecture Notes in Computer Science (including subseries Lecture Notes in Artificial Intelligence and Lecture Notes in Bioinformatics)*, volume 7899 LNCS, pages 64–76.

Alex Lamb, Michael J Paul, and Mark Dredze. 2013. Separating fact from fear: Tracking flu infections on twitter. In *HLT-NAACL*, pages 789–795.

Shen Li, Zhe Zhao, Tao Liu, Renfen Hu, and Xiaoyong Du. 2017. Initializing convolutional filters with semantic features for text classification. In *Proceedings of the 2017 Conference on Empirical Methods in Natural Language Processing*, pages 1884–1889, Copenhagen, Denmark. Association for Computational Linguistics.

Yago Martín, Zhenlong Li, and Susan L. Cutter. 2017. Leveraging twitter to gauge evacuation compliance: Spatiotemporal analysis of hurricane matthew. *PLOS ONE*, 12(7):1–22.

Tomas Mikolov, Kai Chen, Greg Corrado, and Dean Jeffrey. 2013. Efficient estimation of word representations in vector space.

Jeffrey Pennington, Richard Socher, and Christopher D. Manning. 2014. Glove: Global vectors for word representation. In *Empirical Methods in Natural Language Processing (EMNLP)*, pages 1532–1543.

Daniel Preoiuc-Pietro, Ye Liu, Daniel Hopkins, and Lyle Ungar. 2017. Beyond binary labels: Political ideology prediction of twitter users. In *Proceedings of the 55th Annual Meeting of the Association for Computational Linguistics (Volume 1: Long Papers)*, pages 729–740, Vancouver, Canada. Association for Computational Linguistics.

Krishna Chaitanya Sanagavarapu, Alakananda Vempala, and Eduardo Blanco. 2017. Determining whether and when people participate in the events they tweet about. In *Proceedings of the 55th Annual Meeting of the Association for Computational Linguistics (Volume 2: Short Papers)*, pages 641–646, Vancouver, Canada. Association for Computational Linguistics.

Jagan Sankaranarayanan, Hanan Samet, Benjamin E Teitler, Michael D Lieberman, and Jon Sperling. 2009. Twitterstand: news in tweets. In *Proceedings of the 17th acm sigspatial international conference on advances in geographic information systems*, pages 42–51. ACM.

Bharath Sriram, Dave Fuhry, Engin Demir, Hakan Ferhatosmanoglu, and Murat Demirbas. 2010. Short text classification in twitter to improve information filtering. In *Proceedings of the 33rd international ACM SIGIR conference on Research and development in information retrieval*, pages 841–842. ACM.

Kevin Stowe, Michael J. Paul, Martha Palmer, Leysia Palen, and Kenneth Anderson. 2016. Identifying and categorizing disaster-related tweets. In *Proceedings of The Fourth International Workshop on Natural Language Processing for Social Media*, pages 1–6, Austin, TX, USA. Association for Computational Linguistics.

Rachael Tatman, Leo Stewart, Amandalynne Paullada, and Emma Spiro. 2017. Non-lexical features encode political affiliation on twitter. In *Proceedings of the Second Workshop on NLP and Computational Social Science*, pages 63–67, Vancouver, Canada. Association for Computational Linguistics.

Svitlana Volkova, Kyle Shaffer, Jin Yea Jang, and Nathan Hodas. 2017. Separating facts from fiction: Linguistic models to classify suspicious and trusted news posts on twitter. In *Proceedings of the 55th Annual Meeting of the Association for Computational Linguistics (Volume 2: Short Papers)*, pages 647–653, Vancouver, Canada. Association for Computational Linguistics.

Min Yang, Jincheng Mei, Heng Ji, zhao wei, Zhou Zhao, and Xiaojun Chen. 2017. Identifying and tracking sentiments and topics from social media texts during natural disasters. In *Proceedings of the 2017 Conference on Empirical Methods in Natural Language Processing*, pages 527–533, Copenhagen, Denmark. Association for Computational Linguistics.

Political discourse classification in social networks using context sensitive convolutional neural networks

Aritz Bilbao-Jayo
DeustoTech - Fundación Deusto
Avda Universidades, 24,
48007, Bilbao.
aritzbilbao@deusto.es

Aitor Almeida
DeustoTech - Fundación Deusto
Avda Universidades, 24,
48007, Bilbao.
aitor.almeida@deusto.es

Abstract

In this study we propose a new approach to analyse the political discourse in on-line social networks such as Twitter. To do so, we have built a discourse classifier using Convolutional Neural Networks. Our model has been trained using election manifestos annotated manually by political scientists following the Regional Manifestos Project (RMP) methodology. In total, it has been trained with more than 88,000 sentences extracted from more that 100 annotated manifestos. Our approach takes into account the context of the phrase in order to classify it, like what was previously said and the political affiliation of the transmitter. To improve the classification results we have used a simplified political message taxonomy developed within the Electronic Regional Manifestos Project (E-RMP). Using this taxonomy, we have validated our approach analysing the Twitter activity of the main Spanish political parties during 2015 and 2016 Spanish general election and providing a study of their discourse.

1   Introduction

OSN-s are a commonplace element in most citizens daily lives. A significant amount of the social engagement (com, 2015) between citizens takes place in the OSN-s. The same trend is taking place in the political sphere. The on-line presence of political parties and public servants has increased dramatically in the last decades. Political campaigns include an on-line component and politicians use the OSN-s as another medium for their political discourse (Almeida and Orduna, 2017). As a result, the content of the OSN-s can be used to analyse different aspects of the political activity. OSN activity can serve as an input to study the possible results of political campaigns (Kalampokis et al., 2017)(Ortiz-Ángeles et al., 2017), to generate profiles (Grčić et al., 2017) of the politicians according to their OSN usage or to analyse their reactions to certain events or topics (Güneyli et al., 2017).

To take advantage of the political data available in the OSN-s, we present in this paper a deep neural network architecture for political discourse analysis. Our architecture takes advantage of the context of the political discourse (what was previously said and who was the transmitter) to improve the classification process. To do so, we have used the annotated political manifestos database created by the Regional Manifestos Project (RMP) (Alonso et al., 2013). To improve the classification we use the simplified taxonomy that have been developed within the Electronic Regional Manifestos Project (E-RMP), which adapts the initial RMP taxonomy to the political discourse analysis in OSN-s. Using this new taxonomy and the created deep neural network architecture we have analysed the discourse during the electoral campaigns of the 2015 and 2016 Spanish general elections.

This paper is organized as follows. In Section 2 we analyse the previous work done in the area of automatic political discourse analysis in social networks. In Section 3 we describe the classification taxonomy that we have used for the analysis of the political discourse. In Section 4 we present our neural network architecture for political discourse classification. In Section 5 we discuss the evaluation of the system. In Section 6 we offer a real use case of the presented system by analysing the political activity on Twitter during the 2015 and 2016 general elections in Spain. Finally, section 7 draws some conclusions and proposes fur-

Proceedings of the Sixth International Workshop on Natural Language Processing for Social Media , pages 76–85,
Melbourne, Australia, July 20, 2018. ©2018 Association for Computational Linguistics

ther work.

2 Related Work

2.1 Automated use of political manifestos

The automated use of annotated political manifestos as basis for the analysis of other types of political texts besides political manifestos has not been a remarkable research area until recently.

(Nanni et al., 2016) used annotated political manifestos and speeches to analyse the speeches from the las 3 US presidential campaigns in the 7 main domains defined by the manifestos project. The main difference between Nanni et al.'s work and our research is that first, we only use annotated manifestos as training data (while Nanni et al. used annotated speeches too) to later apply this knowledge to another areas such as social networks, and second, this work is applied to analyse the political discourse on social networks and not on political speeches. Moreover, this is the first time that annotated manifestos are used as basis for a political discourse analysis on Twitter to the best of our knowledge.

2.2 Political analysis on Twitter

Since its inception, Twitter has been seen by researchers of several fields as a new source of information where they can conduct their researches. For instance, political scientists have identified Twitter as a platform where they can analyse what a subset of the population says without performing expensive surveys.

Several researchers have measured the predictive power of social networks such as Twitter. (Tumasjan et al., 2010) claimed after analysing more than 100,000 tweets from the 2009th German federal election, that the mere number of messages mentioning a party reflects the election results. Furthermore, (O'Connor et al., 2010) measured the potential Twitter messages might have as a substitute of traditional polling. After using some basic sentiment analysis techniques, O'Connor et al. concluded that a simple sentimental analysis on top of Twitter data produces similar results to polls.

However, there have been diverse criticisms regarding the predictive power of Twitter. For instance, (Gayo Avello et al., 2011) replicated Tumasjan et al.'s and O'Connor's approaches utilising a set of tweets about the 2010 United States House of Representatives elections, obtaining a mean average error of 17.1% compared to election's real results.

The analysis of political polarization in social networks has also been an important research field in political social network analysis. To do so, one of the principal approaches is to construct the graph representation of the social network and apply some network theory principles. On one hand, (Conover et al., 2011) used a combination of community detection algorithms and manually annotated data to analyse the polarity of two networks constructed after gathering more than 250,000 tweets about 2010 U.S congressional midterm elections. The first network represented the retweets and the second one the mentions between different users. Conover et al. concluded that users tend to retweet tweets of users they agree with. Therefore, communities are evident in the retweet network. However, in the mentions network there were more interactions between people with different political ideas, suggesting the existence of discussions between different polarities.

On the other hand, (Finn et al., 2014) introduced a new approach for the measurement of the polarity using a co-retweeted network. The approach was tested with the most retweeted 3,000 tweets within their dataset. Authors concluded that by using their co-retweeted network were able to measure the polarity of the most important accounts participating in the discussion and the polarity of the analysed event.

Other researchers have detected the polarity of raw text using natural language processing techniques. (Iyyer et al., 2014) using recursive neural networks and (Rao and Spasojevic, 2016) using word embeddings and Long Short-Term Memory (LSTM) in order to identify the political polarity of a sentence.

3 Regional Manifestos Project Annotation Taxonomy

Political scientists have been manually annotating political parties' manifestos for years in order to apply content analysis methods and perform political analyses later on.

The precursors of this methodology were the Manifesto Project, formerly known as the Manifesto Research Group (MRG) and Comparative Manifestos previously (CMP)(Budge, 2001). In 2001, they created the Manifesto Coding Handbook(Volkens, 2002) which has evolved over the years. The handbook provides instructions to the annotators about how political parties' manifestos should be coded for later content analysis and a category scheme that indicates the set of codes available for codification. Nowadays, the category scheme for manifestos annotation consists in 56 categories grouped into seven major policy areas (all the categories are available in [1]): *external relations*, *freedom and democracy*, *political system*, *economy*, *welfare and quality of life* and *social groups*.

Moreover, other manifestos annotation projects such as the RMP (the project to which the dataset we have used in this research belongs to) extended the original annotation to address some other political preferences. In particular, they extended the *centralization, decentralization* and *nationalism* categories in order to perform a deeper analysis of those political phenomenons. To do so, they added some new categories to the Manifestos Project category schema, increasing the number of categories from 56 to 78 (the codebook is available at [2]).

However, due to the high number of available categories for annotation, it has been proven that manifestos annotation is not an easy task even for trained political scientists as Mikhaylov et al. demonstrated in (Mikhaylov et al., 2012). The authors concluded after examining diverse annotators' intercoder reliability in two preselected manifestos, that the codification process is highly prone to misclassification due to the large number of categories.

To address the problem that annotating political manifestos is not an easy task even for trained annotators with a codification specifically designed for political manifestos, and to adapt the taxonomy to the political discourse analysis in OSN-s, the E-RMP has developed a simplified taxonomy. This new taxonomy has been created redistributing some of the subdomains of the RMP into new 7 categories: external relations, welfare, economy, democratic regeneration, territorial debate, immigration and boasting. The new distribution of subdomains can be seen in Table 1 and it has been designed in order to analyse European politics. Each of the categories would mean the following:

[1] https://manifesto-project.wzb.eu/coding_schemes/mp_v5
[2] http://www.regionalmanifestosproject.com

- External Relations: references regarding the position/status of the country inside the European Union.

- Welfare: references to welfare state, equality, education, public health, etc.

- Economy: references to any economic sphere of the country.

- Democratic Regeneration: references to the state of democracy, political corruption and new mechanisms of democratic participation.

- Territorial Debate: references to the distribution of power between the state and lower level governments, patriotism, nationalism, pro-independence movements, etc.

- Immigration: references to how immigration should be handled in the country.

- Boasting: references to the speaking party's competence to govern or other party's lack of such competence.

4 Neural Network Architecture for Political Classification

In order to accomplish the text classification task we have opted for convolutional neural networks with Word2Vec word embeddings. Recently, CNNs have achieved excellent results in several text classification tasks (Kim, 2014) and it has been proven their great performance with tweets too(Severyn and Moschitti, 2015).

The inputs of our model are the sentences which are fed to the neural network as sequences of words. These sequences have a maximum length of 60 words (the maximum length have been decided after an analysis of our corpus' sentences' length). Then, this words are mapped to indexes $(1, ..., |D|)$ in a dictionary, being D the number of unique words in the corpus and using the 0 index for padding purposes. After, an embedding layer transforms the word indexes to their corresponding Word2Vec word embeddings. We have opted for the non-static or trainable embedding layer since it improves model's performance. The used Word2Vec model embedding's size is 400 and it has been trained with a corpus of Spanish raw text of 3 billion words(Almeida and Bilbao, 2018).

External Relations	**Economy**
European Integration: Positive	Nationalisation: Positive
European Integration: Negative	Controlled Economy: Positive
Democratic regeneration	Protectionism: Positive
Democracy	Keynesian Demand Management: Positive
Constitutionalism: Positive	Economic Planning: Positive
Representative democracy: Positive	Free-Market Economy: Positive
Participatory democracy: Positive	Economic Orthodoxy: Positive
Political Corruption: Negative	Corporatism: Positive
Immigration	Management of natural resources
Equal treatment of immigrants	Market Regulation: Positive
Welfare expansion for immigrants	Economic Goals
Welfare limitations for immigrants	Incentives: Positive
Education expansion for immigrants	Economic Growth
Education limitation for immigrants	Technology and Infrastructure: Positive
Immigrants' negative impact on law and order	Labour Groups: Positive
Multiculturalism: Positive	Labour Groups: Negative
Territorial Debate	Multiculturalism: Negative
Decentralisation: Positive	**Boasting**
Centralisation: Positive	Political Authority
Regional finance: Positive	**Welfare**
Differential treatment among regions: Negative	Welfare state expansion
Differential treatment among regions: Positive	Education expansion
National Way of Life: Positive	Equality: Positive
Promotion and protection of vernacular languages	
Cultural links with diaspora	
Bilingualism positive	
National way of life: Negative	
Immigrants: Positive	

Table 1: Proposed taxonomy

Once the input phrase has been converted into a sequence of word vectors, the phrase can finally be fed into the convolutional neural network, since the sequence of word vectors are in fact a matrix which dimensions are $60 \times d$ where d is the embedding size. Then, the model performs convolution operations with 3 different filter sizes, batch normalization(Ioffe and Szegedy, 2015) and ReLU as the activation function. Batch normalization acts as an extra regularizer and increases the performance of the model.

As it can be seen in Figure 1, the defined filter sizes are $2 \times d$, $3 \times d$ and $4 \times d$. In other words, these filter sizes define the sizes of the n-grams which in this case are 2-grams, 3-grams and 4-grams respectively. For example, a filter size of $2 \times d$ will take the whole width of all the possible bigrams of the sentence.

Moreover, as it is stated in (Zhang and Wallace, 2015), multiple filters should be used in order to learn complementary features. Therefore, the proposed model has 100 filters per different filter size. Once a filter has been applied, a feature map is generated. Thus, a different feature map is generated per applied filter as it can be seen in Figure 1, where there are 3 filters instead of 100 for explanatory purposes.

After the convolutional neural networks a pooling layer reduces the dimensionality of the incoming data. There are several pooling strategies, however we have opted for the 1-max-pooling(Boureau et al., 2010) strategy since it has been proved in (Zhang and Wallace, 2015) that is the best approach for natural language processing tasks. It captures the most important feature (the highest value) from each of the feature maps. Therefore, the pooling operation outputs a feature per filter which is later concatenated into a feature

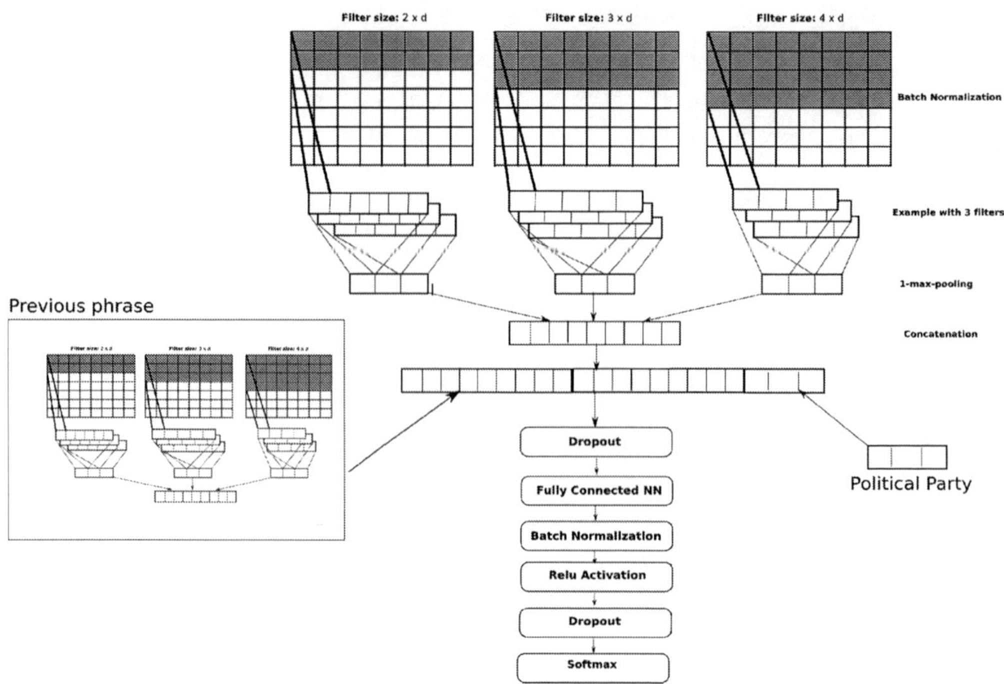

Figure 1: Designed architecture

vector.

Next, a dropout(Srivastava et al., 2014) rate of 0.5 is applied as regularization in order to prevent the network from over-fitting, followed by a fully connected layer with ReLU as the activation function and batch normalization. Then a 0.5 dropout is applied. Finally, the softmax function computes the probability distribution over the labels.

The categorical cross-entropy loss has been used as training objective function since it supports multiclass classifications. Regarding the optimizer, the optimization has been performed using Adam(Kingma and Ba, 2014) with the parameters used in the original manuscript for classification problems.

4.1 Contextual data as new inputs

Two different approaches has been tested in order to insert the previous phrase as an extra input : 1) As a second channel in the convolutional layers. When convolution operations are applied to text only one channel is used. Here we propose the use of an extra channel for the previous context; 2) Replicating for the previous phrase the same convolution-pooling process used for the phrase being classified (see Figure 1).

Regarding the political party, we have decided to represent each political party with a one-hot-encoding representation and concatenate it to the feature maps obtained after the convolutions (see figure 1).

5 Evaluation

The experimentation performed in this research work has been done with the dataset provided by the Regional Manifestos Project, which has a high annotators' intercoder reliability (Alonso et al., 2013). This dataset has almost two decades of political manifestos in Spain and therefore covers a wider span of political issues with a high language variation. The dataset consists in 88,511 annotated phrases and the distribution of codes is highly imbalanced: External Relations (0.9%), Welfare (35.91%), Economy (47.83%), Democratic Regeneration (4.38%), Immigration (1.77%), Territorial debate (7.81%), Boasting (1.3%). Almost 85% of the dataset belongs to Welfare and Economy categories, leaving around the 15% of the dataset for the remaining 5 categories.

In order to evaluate our approach, we have divided our dataset in 2 different subsets: training and validation sets (85%), and test set (15%). The training and validation set has been used in order to create models with 5-fold cross validation to

Experiment	Accuracy	F1(Macro)
E1	83.79%	69.19
E2	83.8%	69.64
E3	86.36%	72.58
E4	**87.63%**	**75.29**
E5	87.55%	74.68

Table 2: Results with political manifestos.

Experiment	Accuracy	F1(Macro)
T1	67.57%	57.07
T2	69.05%	63.06
T3	66.33%	60.26
T4	**70.59%**	**63.17**

Table 3: Results with annotated tweets.

later test their performance with the same test set. The reason why we have split the dataset in 2 subsets and then apply cross-validation to one of them is because we have used early stopping (Prechelt, 1998) in order to stop our model's training when it started to over-fit. Early stopping compares the training accuracy with the validation accuracy and after some epochs without any improvements in the validation accuracy it stops the training. Nevertheless, the model may have over-fitted with respect to the validation set, therefore, a third set (test set) is needed in order to measure the real performance of the model. Furthermore, since we work with an imbalanced dataset, we have applied stratification in order to preserve the same percentage of samples for each class. Using this approach we are able to evaluate how each class is classified since it ensures that in each of the subsets there will be a representation of each class. Taking into account both the high number of classes and the imbalance between them, we have used the f-measure as the evaluation metric. Additionally we also provide the accuracy of each experiment.

We have performed five different experiments to analyse the importance of the context (both the what was said previously and who is saying it) when classifying the political discourse: 1) Only the sentence to be classified with no additional context (*E1*); 2) the sentence plus the political party who belongs to (*E2*); 3) the sentence plus the previous sentence in an additional channel on the CNNs (*E3*); 4) the sentence plus the previous sentence in another CNNs structure, concatenating the features extracted by both networks (*E4*); and 5) the sentence, the political party who belongs to and the previous sentence in another CNN(*E5*).

As it is shown in table 2, the performance of the classifiers improves when adding the previous sentence and the political party as extra features. On the one hand, the previous sentence provides a remarkable increase in accuracy and F1 when it is inserted as an additional channel on the CNNs

(E3) and as as a new structure of CNNs (E4). However, the improvement in E4 is greater than in E3. On the other hand, adding the political party who says the phrase as an extra feature (E2) improves the F1 in 0.45 points compared with the baseline (E1). With regard to E5, since combining party and previous phrase does not improve the results of E4, we can affirm that those two features are not complementary.

Additionally, we have also tested the performance of our model on Twitter. To do so, we have tested the aforementioned models in a dataset of 404 manually annotated tweets. The category distribution of the test set is the following one: external relations (0.74%), welfare(33.66%), economy(30.69%), democratic regeneration(14.35%), immigration(0.49%), territorial debate(16.58%), boasting(3.46%).

It is important to remark that these models have been trained using the annotated manifestos from the Regional Manifestos Project dataset, without using any tweet during the training process.

We have performed four different experiments to analyse the performance of the previously explained architecture when classifying manually annotated tweets: 1) Only the tweet to be classified with no additional context and a Word2Vec model generated with generic Spanish text (*T1*); 2) the tweet to be classified with no additional context and a Word2Vec model generated with generic Spanish text and on-line trained with the tweets of our Spanish elections dataset (*T2*); 3) the tweet to be classified with the tweet it is answering to in another CNNs structure and a Word2Vec model generated with generic Spanish text (*T3*); 4) the tweet to be classified with the tweet it is answering to in another CNNs structure and a Word2Vec model generated with generic Spanish text and on-line trained with the tweets of our Spanish elections dataset (*T4*).

As it can be seen in table 3, retraining the Word2Vec model with tweets of our Spanish elections dataset significantly increases the accuracy and F-measure of the model. On the one hand, from T1 to T2 there is an improvement of 2.5 points in accuracy and 6 points in F1. On the other hand, from T3 to T4 there is an improvement of 4 points in accuracy and 3 points in F1. With regard to the use of the previous tweet in the thread, it improves the accuracy of the model in 1.5 points.

6 Use Case

To demonstrate the usefulness of our system, we present a possible use case scenario for our classification model: to analyse the political discourse of the Spanish political parties and candidates during the campaign period of the 2015 and 2016 Spanish general elections on Twitter. In Spain, general elections should be held every 4 years. However, after the results of 2015 Spanish general elections neither of the two most voted parties were capable of obtaining the necessary support to form a government. Therefore, after months of unsuccessful negotiations new general elections were called.

The performed analysis consists in classifying the tweets written by the political parties standing for elections in the previously mentioned 7 categories to later analyse how some political parties prioritise some categories over others. To do so, we gathered from 4th to 18th of December (the 2015 general election was held on the 20th of December) (Almeida et al., 2015) and from 10th to 24th of June (the 2016 general election was held on the 26th of June) (Almeida et al., 2016) all the tweets written by the political parties and candidates standing for election. We gathered more than 80,000 tweets (taking into account both elections) from more than 10 different political parties and their respective candidates.

In order to perform the political discourse analysis, we used the previously mentioned classification model to distribute the tweets from 5 political parties (ignoring retweets) in the 7 categories previously defined. The analysed political parties are:

- People's Party (PP): right-wing, conservative political party. PP had been the ruling party between 2011-2015 having an absolute majority in Parliament.

- Spanish Socialist Workers' Party (PSOE): social democratic, centre-left political party. PSOE had been the ruling party between (2004-2011) when due to the financial crisis

and the high unemployment rate in Spain lost the 2011 Spanish general elections.

- Podemos - We Can: left-wing political party. The party was founded in 2014 and their main objectives where to address unemployment, inequality, corruption and austerity problems.

- Citizens: centre, liberal political party. Even though it was founded in 2006 as regional party in Catalonia, the party started to have influence at national level in the end of 2014.

- Basque Nationalist Party (PNV): centre-right, Christian democratic, Basque nationalist party.

6.1 2015 general elections political discourse analysis

In figure 2, the distribution of the tweets of the 5 analysed Spanish political parties over the 7 categories is shown. On the one thand, the first worth mentioning aspect is how *Boasting* is the dominant category on the 4 main political parties running for the 2015 general elections in all regions of Spain (People's Party, Spanish Socialist Workers' Party - PSOE, Podemos - We Can, Citizens). Moreover, it is also remarkable that People's party, the ruling party when the elections were held, is the political party with the highest percentage in *Boasting*. On the other hand, the Basque Nationalist Party (PNV) focuses its discourse on *Territorial Debate* category. This category includes topics such as the distribution of power between state and lower level governments (Basque Nationalists want more autonomy for their region), promotion and protection of vernacular language such as Basque, bilingualism (in Basque Country there are two official languages: Spanish and Basque) or nationalism which in this case would be Basque nationalism.

It is also noteworthy how differently the two main Spanish political parties (PP and PSOE) prioritised *Welfare* category. The low interest shown by the People's Party on *Welfare* may be due to the austerity measures taken and the performed cutbacks in the welfare state and social protection during their period as the ruling party. Therefore, it would make sense to assume that PSOE (the first opposition party) could see this as an opportunity to take advantage to differentiate themselves from the People's Party. However, People's Party is not the political party which has talked less about Welfare and Quality of Life. As it can be seen in Figure 2, Citizens talks even less about Welfare and Quality of Life which may be related to their liberal ideology.

With regard to *Democratic regeneration*, it is clearly seen in figure 2 that mainly Citizens, but also Podemos- We can and Spanish Socialist Workers' Party - PSOE, gave a high importance to this category, unlike PP. *Democratic regeneration* encompasses concepts such as calls for constitutional amendments or changes, favourable mentions of the system of direct democracy, the need of involvement of all citizens in political decision-making, division of powers, independence of courts, etc. These concepts were introduced in Spanish politics after 2011 15-M Movement (Hughes, 2011), and continued to gain in importance during the legislature, being one of the main topics the parties on the opposition addressed during their campaign.

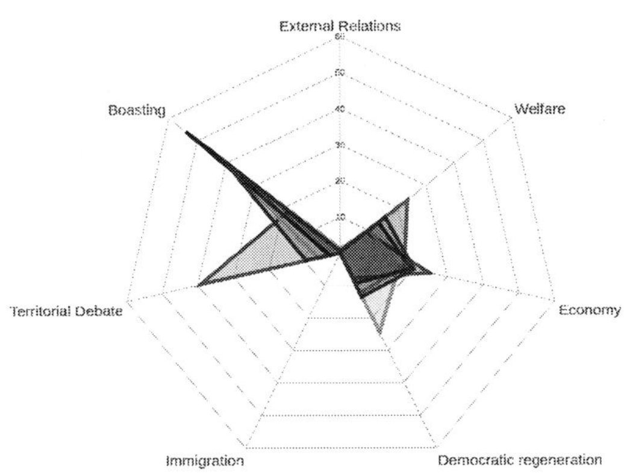

Figure 2: Distribution among 7 categories of the tweets created by the Twitter accounts of PSOE (red), PP (Blue), Podemos - We Can (Purple), Citizens (Orange) and PNV (Green) in 2015 Spanish general elections

6.2 2016 general elections political discourse analysis

One relevant change in the 2016 elections political discourse in Twitter is the use of *External Relations* category. In the previous elections this domain was ignored by all the political parties. However, as it can be seen in figure 3, People's Party and Citizens emphasized more this category than in the previous general elections. This could have happened due to Brexit.

With respect to the rest of categories, it is noteworthy how the 4 main political parties gave less importance to *Boasting* category in favour of *Democratic regeneration* and *Economy*.

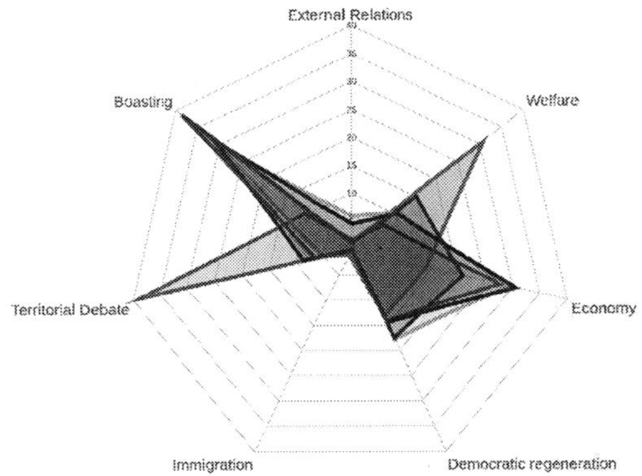

Figure 3: Distribution among 7 categories of the tweets created by the Twitter accounts of PSOE (red), PP (Blue), Podemos - We Can (Purple), Citizens (Orange) and PNV (Green) in 2016 Spanish general elections

7 Conclusions and Future Work

In this paper we present a model, based in a convolutional neural network architecture, which takes advantage of the context to classify the political discourse in OSN-s. The political discourse classification is based in a simplified taxonomy developed within the Electronic Regional Manifestos Project, which has been created to be applied specifically to OSN-s. To demonstrate the utility of our model we have used it to analyse the Twitter activity of the main political parties during the 2015 and 2016 Spanish general elections. The proposed model can be easily retrained to work in other languages, using the for example the dataset of the Manifesto Project[3], which provides annotated manifestos in several languages.

As future work, we would like to study how attention mechanisms (Hermann et al., 2015) could be used to improved the classification process, in order to obtain better results. We would also like to take advantage of the inner representation created by the capsule networks(Sabour et al., 2017) to create vectors that represent each one of the target categories, in order to use them for the classification.

---

[3]https://manifesto-project.wzb.eu/

Acknowledgments

We gratefully acknowledge the support of the Basque Government's Department of Education for the predoctoral funding; the Ministry of Economy, Industry and Competitiveness of Spain under Grant No. CSO2015-64495-R (Electronic Regional Manifestos Project); and NVIDIA Corporation with the donation of the Titan X used for this research. We thank the Regional Manifestos Project team (Braulio Gómez Fortes and Matthias Scantamburlo) for making available their dataset of annotated political manifestos and tweets.

References

2015. Media metrix cross-platform. Technical report, comScore.

Aitor Almeida and Aritz Bilbao. 2018. Spanish 3b words word2vec embeddings.

Aitor Almeida, Pablo Orduña, and Aritz Bilbao. 2015. Party and candidate tweets for the campaign period of the 2015 spanish general election.

Aitor Almeida, Pablo Orduña, and Aritz Bilbao. 2016. Party and candidate tweets for the campaign period of the 2016 spanish general election.

Aitor Almeida and Pablo Orduna. 2017. Analyzing political discourse in on-line social networks j. ucs special issue. *Journal of Universal Computer Science*, 23(3):233–235.

Sonia Alonso, Braulio Gómez, and Laura Cabeza. 2013. Measuring centre–periphery preferences: The regional manifestos project. *Regional & Federal Studies*, 23(2):189–211.

Y-Lan Boureau, Jean Ponce, and Yann LeCun. 2010. A theoretical analysis of feature pooling in visual recognition. In *Proceedings of the 27th international conference on machine learning (ICML-10)*, pages 111–118.

Ian Budge. 2001. *Mapping policy preferences: estimates for parties, electors, and governments, 1945-1998*, volume 1. Oxford University Press on Demand.

Michael Conover, Jacob Ratkiewicz, Matthew R Francisco, Bruno Gonçalves, Filippo Menczer, and Alessandro Flammini. 2011. Political polarization on twitter. *ICWSM*, 133:89–96.

Samantha Finn, Eni Mustafaraj, and P Takis Metaxas. 2014. The co-retweeted network and its applications for measuring the perceived political polarization.

Daniel Gayo Avello, Panagiotis T Metaxas, and Eni Mustafaraj. 2011. Limits of electoral predictions using twitter. In *Proceedings of the Fifth International AAAI Conference on Weblogs and Social Media*. Association for the Advancement of Artificial Intelligence.

Klara Grčić, Marina Bagić Babac, and Vedran Podobnik. 2017. Generating politician profiles based on content analysis of social network datasets. *Journal of Universal Computer Science*, 23(3):236–255.

Ahmet Güneyli, Metin Ersoy, and Sevki Kiralp. 2017. Terrorism in the 2015 election period in turkey: Content analysis of political leaders' social media activity. *J. UCS*, 23(3):256–279.

Karl Moritz Hermann, Tomas Kocisky, Edward Grefenstette, Lasse Espeholt, Will Kay, Mustafa Suleyman, and Phil Blunsom. 2015. Teaching machines to read and comprehend. In *Advances in Neural Information Processing Systems*, pages 1693–1701.

Neil Hughes. 2011. young people took to the streets and all of a sudden all of the political parties got old: The 15m movement in spain. *Social Movement Studies*, 10(4):407–413.

Sergey Ioffe and Christian Szegedy. 2015. Batch normalization: Accelerating deep network training by reducing internal covariate shift. *arXiv preprint arXiv:1502.03167*.

Mohit Iyyer, Peter Enns, Jordan Boyd-Graber, and Philip Resnik. 2014. Political ideology detection using recursive neural networks. In *Proceedings of the Association for Computational Linguistics*, pages 1113–1122.

Evangelos Kalampokis, Areti Karamanou, Efthimios Tambouris, and Konstantinos A Tarabanis. 2017. On predicting election results using twitter and linked open data: The case of the uk 2010 election. *J. UCS*, 23(3):280–303.

Yoon Kim. 2014. Convolutional neural networks for sentence classification. *arXiv preprint arXiv:1408.5882*.

Diederik Kingma and Jimmy Ba. 2014. Adam: A method for stochastic optimization. *arXiv preprint arXiv:1412.6980*.

Slava Mikhaylov, Michael Laver, and Kenneth R Benoit. 2012. Coder reliability and misclassification in the human coding of party manifestos. *Political Analysis*, 20(1):78–91.

Federico Nanni, Cäcilia Zirn, Goran Glavas, Jason Eichorst, and Simone Paolo Ponzetto. 2016. Topfish: Topic-based analysis of political position in us electoral campaigns.

Brendan O'Connor, Ramnath Balasubramanyan, Bryan R Routledge, and Noah A Smith. 2010. From tweets to polls: Linking text sentiment to public opinion time series. *ICWSM*, 11(122-129):1–2.

Sonia Ortiz-Ángeles, Yenny Villuendas-Rey, Itzamá López-Yáñez, Oscar Camacho-Nieto, and Cornelio Yáñez-Márquez. 2017. Electoral preferences prediction of the yougov social network users based on computational intelligence algorithms. *J. UCS*, 23(3):304–326.

Lutz Prechelt. 1998. Early stopping-but when? In *Neural Networks: Tricks of the trade*, pages 55–69. Springer.

Adithya Rao and Nemanja Spasojevic. 2016. Actionable and political text classification using word embeddings and lstm. *arXiv preprint arXiv:1607.02501*.

Sara Sabour, Nicholas Frosst, and Geoffrey E Hinton. 2017. Dynamic routing between capsules. In *Advances in Neural Information Processing Systems*, pages 3859–3869.

Aliaksei Severyn and Alessandro Moschitti. 2015. Twitter sentiment analysis with deep convolutional neural networks. In *Proceedings of the 38th International ACM SIGIR Conference on Research and Development in Information Retrieval*, pages 959–962. ACM.

Nitish Srivastava, Geoffrey E Hinton, Alex Krizhevsky, Ilya Sutskever, and Ruslan Salakhutdinov. 2014. Dropout: a simple way to prevent neural networks from overfitting. *Journal of Machine Learning Research*, 15(1):1929–1958.

Andranik Tumasjan, Timm Oliver Sprenger, Philipp G Sandner, and Isabell M Welpe. 2010. Predicting elections with twitter: What 140 characters reveal about political sentiment.

Andrea Volkens. 2002. Manifesto coding instructions.

Ye Zhang and Byron Wallace. 2015. A sensitivity analysis of (and practitioners' guide to) convolutional neural networks for sentence classification. *arXiv preprint arXiv:1510.03820*.

Author Index